LITTLE PANCHO

LITTLE PANCHO

The Life of Tennis Legend
Pancho Segura

CAROLINE SEEBOHM

UNIVERSITY OF NEBRASKA PRESS ○ LINCOLN AND LONDON

Library of Congress Cataloging-in-Publication Data

Seebohm, Caroline.
Little Pancho : the life of tennis legend Pancho
Segura / Caroline Seebohm.
   p. cm.
Includes bibliographical references and index.
ISBN 978-0-8032-2041-6 (cloth : alk. paper)
1. Segura, Pancho. 2. Tennis Players—Ecuador—
Biography. 3. Tennis players—United States—
Biography. I. Title.
GV994.S44S43 2009   796.342092—dc22
[B]   2008047511

Set in Scala and Scala Sans by Kim Essman.
Designed by A. Shahan.

Contents

Prologue A Match to Remember

Like all great contests, it pits David versus Goliath. Pancho Segura, the little guy, five foot six, bandy-legged, pigeon-toed, with dark Indian looks reminiscent of the ancient tribes of South America, blessed with phenomenal speed and a devastating two-handed forehand, against Pancho Gonzales, the tall, lithe, movie-star-handsome Mexican-American, younger by seven years, moody and reckless in his often-troubled journey to the top of the sport.

Both are called Pancho—the name white Americans in those days gave to anyone south of the border, probably thinking of the only Latino they were familiar with—Pancho Villa, the famous Mexican freedom fighter. "I didn't mind," Segura said. Gonzales did.

The date is July 5, 1951. The place is the top tennis arena in the United States—the West Side Tennis Club at Forest Hills, in Queens, New York. The surface is grass, the traditional surface for the game of tennis, and for many players the most challenging—fast, tricky, risky, beautiful. The tournament is a round-robin, popular with audiences who like to see their favorite players play several matches, rather than knockout rounds that ensure quick elimination.

The two men have played each other several times before, but this is their first meeting on grass. Segura, at the age of thirty-one, is playing his best tennis. He holds the U.S. Pro title, having a year earlier in Cleveland triumphed over the impossible-to-beat king of the "big game" Jack Kramer, considered the best player on the circuit and the defending professional champion. As for his opponent, after a stop-and-start career as a pro, Gonzales, now twenty-four, is starting to show his true brilliance, and fans have begun to sense that at some point in the near future this ferociously aggressive tennis player will attain the highest level in the game.

Segura comes into the match without having lost a set in his four other round-robin contests in this Forest Hills tournament. Gonzales has won three out of four. The numbers favor Segura, but Gonzales's size, athleticism, and power make the odds less certain. Gonzales defeated Segura in a round-robin earlier this year in Philadelphia and is ahead of him in the pro standings going into this tournament. The contrast in their physical appearance is stark. Nobody is certain how well Little Pancho, in spite of his triumphs, can compensate for his obvious disadvantages.

The match is called for early afternoon. It's been raining, the recurring menace for grass-court players, who must not only cope with irregular bounces and slippery hitting conditions but also the ever-present danger of falling and causing serious physical injury. Four thousand fans sit huddled in the stands, knowing that this duel will offer spectacular tennis between two delightfully mismatched physical specimens. Old-timers are reminded of the great contests in the early 1920s between "Big Bill" Tilden, at just over six foot one the tallest player in the game, and his constant rival, "Little Bill" Johnston, at five foot eight a lightweight by comparison, whose speed and skill were usually defeated in the end by Tilden's superior psychological and physical strength.

Sports fans love an underdog, and like Johnston, Segura arouses the passionate support of the crowd with his underdog's arsenal—the "sneaky" shots that work their magic to get his opponents out of position, the lapidary two-handed forehand that is so accurate that it could knock over a single nail on the other side of the net, the almost supernatural anticipation that takes the momentum away from an opponent's hard-hit ball that looks like a winner. When he pulls off one of his disguised drop shots that leaves the other player stranded in confusion, the Inca Warrior, as sportswriters call him, looks up at the stands and taps his finger to his brain with a delighted smile. The fans go wild.

On this wet, momentous day, Gonzales comes out swinging. His famous huge serve-and-volley game is quickly put to the test, however, by the slippery court and Segura's quicksilver response. Segura's return of serve—that most challenging and vital of shots—is relentless, putting Gonzales back on his heels. Segura's own serve, not as powerful a weapon as that of others on the tour, on this day is laser-sharp, sending Gonzales into corners that he can't scramble out of, or pinning the Mexican-American in the center of the box where he is defenseless. Perhaps the most striking element of the match, however, is Segura's speed. The tricky surface seems not only not to slow him down but actually to inject his legs with an unexpected and ardent energy. As the match progresses, Gonzales begins to look like an aging bumblebee beside this sparkling firefly of an opponent.

"I flew," Pancho Segura concedes afterward with a smile.

First set, 6–3. Second set, 6–4. Now the fans are smelling victory for the "little dynamo." Segura continues to minimize his errors, while Gonzales, angered and frustrated, begins to miss shots. It is now that Big Pancho fatally loses confidence and stays back on the baseline. At this critical moment, he chooses to avoid risk at the net, normally the most successful offensive position on grass, and where he is usually so dominating.

Segura, that most intelligent of players, knows very well what this means and takes quick advantage, drilling his forehand past the bigger man with the accuracy of a diamond cutter, mixing it up with cunning drop shots, placing his backhands with such blistering clarity that Gonzales is unable to respond effectively. Segura not only miraculously saves some of Gonzales's best smashes but turns them into winning points. No one has ever disputed Gonzales's fighting spirit, and he has turned many likely defeats into triumphs. But this time, as the third set spirals out of control, he can do nothing to save it. Segura is invincible and wins the last set 6–2. The match is over in an hour.

The sports reporters covering the match were awed by Little Pancho's victory. Legendary tennis writer Allison Danzig, writing in the *New York Times*, said that "Segura extracted the sting from Gonzales's potent service and net attack with the virulence and accuracy of his calculated counter-measures until the big Californian was all but helpless under the relentless pressure on the wet turf in the final set." Jesse Abramson of the *New York Herald Tribune* was no less impressed, describing "gritty and skilful" Segura "mowing down" Gonzales. "[He] outsteadied his taller foe from the baseline and frequently outplayed the mercurial Gonzales at the net. . . . His speed and court coverage and unbreakable defense were too much for Gonzales."

Insiders knew that Segura's performance was no surprise that afternoon at Forest Hills. They knew how his mind worked in a match, how his speed and anticipation worked for him on the testing grass surface, how his physical and psychological approach to tennis made him one of the most original players in the history of the game. They knew how well he had done his homework, studying Gonzales's racket work and tirelessly practicing the shots that would cause the bigger and stronger man to flounder. But for many that day, watching the small, skinny, bowlegged Ecuadorian explode against the athletically gifted, towering Californian, they felt they were watching a rare comet streaking across the rain-dark sky. The final score was unimaginable. Not worth even a minimal bet. Segura was never supposed to win the match against Gonzales that afternoon. Yet he killed him in three short sets. How did it happen?

LITTLE PANCHO

Chapter One Miracle in Ecuador

Nobody noticed the small dark-skinned boy in a corner of the Guayaquil Tennis Club, hitting ball after ball against the wall with a dilapidated-looking tennis racket. The boy was alarmingly thin, with bandy, skinny legs that curved in like bananas, and slender arms with fragile wrists, so fragile that in order to stroke the ball hard enough for it to bounce back from the wall, he had to keep both hands on the handle of the racket. To the few members of the club who might have glanced at him as they left the court and prepared to go back to their expensive homes for a shower and a drink, he was just another poor little kid from the barrio who was passing the time while waiting for somebody to take him home.

They would have been mistaken, and if they had paused to look at the little boy more carefully, they might have realized their mistake. For the child's expression was one of fierce concentration and focus. He was not just passing the time. He was practicing hitting tennis balls the only way he knew how—by doing it over and over again with a passion that belied his young age. What was reflected in that boy's eager, intent face was what audiences all over the world would come to know and thrill to one day.

As it grew dark at the club and long shadows made it difficult for the boy to see the ball anymore, a tall, strongly built man came from the courts where he had been tidying up, collecting towels and balls, unwinding the nets, locking doors, and closing up the club. "Panchito, *vamos a la casa.* Let's go home."

Reluctantly, the little boy stopped his hitting, picked up the ball he had been playing with, gave it to his father, and took his hand. It was time for Domingo and Pancho Segura Cano to go home.

Francisco—Pancho—Segura (Cano was his mother's name, commonly used as the family name in Latin American countries) was about seven years old when he first picked up a tennis racket. By this time he had already been through illnesses and hardships that might have deterred a less determined character. He was born on June 20, 1921, on a bus traveling from Quevedo to Guayaquil. "The roads at that time were in bad condition," remembered Francisca Cano de Segura, Pancho's mother. "We had gone a short way when I had to ask my husband to ask the bus driver, as a favor, to return to Quevedo because I was going to give birth prematurely." Thus "the little dark one" (*morenito*), as his mother called him, entered the world.

There was nothing romantic about his birth. He was the firstborn son of Domingo Segura Paredes and Francisca Cano. His father was Spanish in origin, his mother an Indian from Quevedo, so their son was technically a *cholo*, of mixed blood. He was born in June, which in some parts of the world is a lovely month, with clear blue skies and gardens in bloom. In Guayaquil it is wretchedly hot and only a little less humid than in the officially rainy months, December through April. From his very first moments, Pancho, like everyone else in Guayaquil, had to learn to accommodate to the heavy, sticky, mosquito-infested air of his native city.

Guayaquil in the 1900s was a modest commercial city of roughly 250,000 people, located in a sweltering region of the southern coast not far from the Peruvian border. In those days it had a third-world look, with small wooden houses with corrugated iron roofs, dusty streets with horses and carts, very few cars, and untended vegetation. After a devastating series of fires, most of the new houses built in the city were built of cement.

Its primary source of employment was the port, which was the major shipping entry into Ecuador through the El Salado estuary, transporting cargo in and out of this small South American country nestled in the Andes. The Guayas River delta is the largest in the southern Pacific, and the maritime port still handles three-quarters of the country's imports and almost half of its exports. Most of the inhabitants of Guayaquil who made money in those years had import-export businesses, trading in such goods as coffee and bananas. They lived in large houses to the north of the city, surrounded by high walls and flowering trees, and belonged to the Union Club, with its fine view of the waterfront. It was gentlemen like these who founded the first Guayaquil Tennis Club in 1910.

Apart from the fine houses owned by the rich, perhaps the most compelling aspect of Guayaquil was—and still is—its cemetery. Positioned on a hill above the city, it is the place where for well over a century hundreds of thousands of Guayaquil's citizens have been laid to rest. The grand residents of the town are buried in an extended plateau within the city's gates at the bottom of the hill, where the imposing mausoleums, handsome statuary, and sculptures reflect the importance of the departed they so impressively memorialize. Rising up the hill in an increasingly crowded jumble, the cemetery becomes more democratic, a *ciudad blanco*, or white city, inhabited by the local dead, a poignant mass of disorderly, crumbling, packed-together crosses and shrines, almost uniformly painted white, with black inscriptions. Pancho Segura's parents are buried there.

In 1921, Guayaquil remained a place where long life was in short supply. Pancho was the first of seven children (two more boys and four girls came later) born to Domingo and Francisca. (There was also a daughter from Domingo's first marriage.) Nothing came easily to them. But the eldest son, Francisco, seemed to attract the most difficult challenges. His childhood was riddled with sickness. The first major illness he suffered was a double hernia, an affliction fairly common in baby boys. A pediatric hernia is related to the development and descent of the testes and causes acute swelling and pain in the groin. It is likely that Pancho's parents did not immediately recognize the problem, and allowed it to go untreated. By the age of ten, Pancho remembered being almost unable to walk, the pain and swelling were so great. He was finally operated on and the hernia was removed.

Another hazard for those living in the Ecuadorian climate was malaria, a disease endemic to travelers in the tropics. Mosquitoes were a permanent threat in Guayaquil, both outside and in, for with no air-conditioning, windows had always to be kept open to capture the faintest breeze. Pancho caught malaria when he was eight or nine, and suffered from it intermittently until he was twenty. Malaria brings debilitating fever and weakness in the patient, and Pancho was often in bed with this recurring illness. Once he had to go to the hospital for a "quinine cure," where he lay ravaged by "the shakes," his mother sitting by anxiously.

But the most serious affliction endured by the young Ecuadorian was rickets. Rickets is a childhood disorder caused by malnutrition, in particular the lack of vitamin C, calcium, and phosphate. Mercifully rare in developed countries, rickets causes skeletal deformities, most commonly bowlegs, Pancho's own disability. It is hard to know what kind of food Pancho and his family ate, but the incidence of rickets shows that poverty played a large role in their struggle to survive. Pancho had rickets because as a young child he did not have an adequate diet, and his body never forgave him.

Pancho's father, Domingo Cano, provided as best he could for his growing family. A handsome, strong man, six-feet-two-inches tall, he worked as guardian to the property of one of the wealthiest men in Guayaquil, Don Juan José Medina. Medina, who had been educated in England and was an important banker in town, became *padrino*, or godfather to little Pancho. Medina was very concerned about the boy's development and thought Pancho should take up an activity that would strengthen his bones, fill out his muscles, and add much-needed bulk to the child's stunted frame. Medina decided that that activity should be his own favorite sport—the game of tennis.

Señor Medina was on the board of the Guayaquil Tennis Club, a small, elite club that consisted of only five hundred members. In Ecuador, indeed all over the world, tennis was considered an upper-class sport, a rich man's game, available only to those who could afford to spend their leisure time using expensively made rackets to hit expensively produced balls at each other across expensively woven nets on expensively cared-for surfaces in expensively maintained clubs while wearing expensive, long, white trousers and expensive white sweaters and expensively designed shoes.

Medina decided to hire Domingo Cano to be caretaker of the Guayaquil Tennis Club. This position gave Cano not only a regular salary but also lodging. The family was given a small house on the tennis club grounds. In return, Cano was to look after the courts, maintain the grounds and the clubhouse, and provide services for the members including, perhaps most importantly for tennis players, ball boys. Panchito would become, in effect, assistant to his father, and at the same time start to play tennis.

It was an entirely private arrangement, of course. The club members did not see or think much about their staff. As long as the club and the courts were kept in tip-top shape, and there were ball boys to pick up the balls, who actually did these jobs was not of much concern. Pancho, like three or four other little boys hired by the club, scurried about collecting balls and throwing them when required to the players, otherwise making themselves as invisible as possible. Pancho was the youngest. "My dad had me picking up balls, brushing the lines, fixing the net, handing towels to members," Pancho recalled. The club had only four courts, all cement, which were mostly busy on weekends when the members were not at work, but Pancho would come every day after school to help his father.

In elementary school in Guayaquil, Pancho was a good student, particularly in mathematics. "I was good at numbers." He had good teachers. But he was lonely. Because he was so frail and undersized, his schoolmates teased him unmercifully and called him *maricon*, fairy. Every day after school, instead of playing sports or simply hanging out with friends, he went to the tennis club, a place off-limits to his classmates. It was an isolated life for a child.

One day, inevitably, he picked up a tennis racket. It was old, abandoned, thrown out by one of the members. It was far too big for him. He almost had to lift it with both hands, let alone try to hit the ball with it. But Pancho put his hands round the handle, bounced a ball, and swiped. "At the beginning, I wasn't interested," he remembered. "All my friends at school played soccer. But when I hit the ball against a wall, I liked it."

There were perhaps other forces at play here. Pancho was small and weak for his age at school. He could not play sports as well as his classmates. While they played soccer and baseball, Pancho was often on the sidelines. Tennis, this mysterious game that his school friends knew nothing about, was something Pancho could learn privately, with his father, at the club. When the courts were empty, his father would pick up a racket and take his son to hit with him sometimes. "We'd sneak on to the courts."

His mother, however, was the athlete in the family. (It was not only Pancho who inherited her genes. Pancho's sister, Elvira, became a national champion basketball player.) Francisca Cano would also play tennis with Panchito, and for a while, she beat him. "He hated it so much, finally she let him beat her," Elvira remembered.

But tennis was not what Francisca wanted for her son. (Neither was basketball what she wanted for her daughter. She expected her five girls to stay home, to help in the house, and prepare for good marriages.) Pancho's mother felt uneasy about her son's growing passion for tennis—it kept him away from the house, away from her. Her firstborn, he was made even more precious to her by his frailty. (Both his brothers grew to be over six feet tall.) She nurtured him, cared for him, nursed him, prayed for him. She loved her other children as attentively, even binding her daughters' legs as infants in order to fend off the distressing bowlegged legacy of her eldest son.

But Panchito, being the most vulnerable, was perhaps her favorite. Very religious, Señora Cano wanted him to be more religious also, and made him take his sisters to novenas. She insisted that every time they passed a church he go in and take the holy water.

She was also the disciplinarian in the family. "She used to give us the belt," Elvira said. "I remember Pancho objecting, saying '*Mama*, you're going to hit a tennis champion?'"

Pancho's mother would go to the courts with her son, but she often found the situation distressing. He did not have proper tennis shoes; they were made from rubber tires. His socks were not long and white, like those of the other players. She could not afford such luxuries for her son. But there were worse things. She saw how her boy was treated by the club members when he was working as a ball boy, clearly recalling it all at the end of her life. "I remember one game when he sat on the chair of one of the *señores*. 'What the hell are you doing sitting there?' he asked. 'You have to sit over there, on the stairs.' And so my son left quietly, to sit on the stairs. He was also forbidden to use the bathroom of the *señores*. But he, with a good sense of humor, used to tell me, 'They tell me not to use their chairs or their bathroom, but when they are not there I sit and I shower as many times as I want to . . . and some day I will be sitting in those seats right in front of all of them.'"

So his mother grew to accept her son's ambition and passion for the game. As he grew older, she was drawn into his obsession and began to encourage him. She would come to the club at twilight, after all the members had gone home, and take Pancho on to the empty courts, hitting back and forth with her tireless son. Once he became a teenager, there was no question of who was beating whom. They would play until it was too dark to see the ball. How he resented that coming of darkness. "I remember he would cry because he couldn't play in the daytime," his sister Elvira said, "only at night."

While Pancho was the eldest son and favorite of his mother, he was also the most responsible in temperament. As is often the case with the eldest son, he was acutely aware of his position in the family. As a child, he would take a burro into the hillsides outside the city and bring back firewood. "There were times when my son brought home up to one *sucre* that he had earned during the day," his mother announced proudly. There was nothing he would not do to help his parents, brothers, and sisters, an impulse and a duty that later proved both complex and, in some ways, tragic. He left school completely after two years, to work for his family. It was a painful decision. He was twelve years old.

He admitted later that his childhood was sad, because his life at the club, and leaving school early, separated him from his friends. "They weren't allowed there. It was a private club, and we were just servants. I couldn't get them in." The lack of money also isolated him. "I never had a bike. I couldn't go anywhere, not even to the beach."

Because of the family's poverty, the larger world was closed to him. "In those days," he said, laughing at the recollection, "if we saw a plane we thought it was a bird!" He would look longingly at the magnificent Grace Line ships that sailed in and out of the port of Guayaquil. How unthinkable it was to him that he would ever be able to afford to travel on one of those huge liners. Sleek, glamorous, they tantalized the boy with their noisy sirens, full of empty promises. How often did he wistfully dream that one day he might escape from Guayaquil on one of those Grace Line steamers. "Some day I will go on a boat like that away from here," he would promise himself. "One day I will become somebody."

Meanwhile, there was no alternative for him except to go on hitting balls against the wall at the Guayaquil Tennis Club. He began to commit himself more and more to learning about the game. Although he saw that all the grown-up players at the club used one-handed forehands and backhands, he found he could hit more powerfully by continuing to use both hands on his forehand. (It wasn't until the 1960s that players began to use both hands for forehand and backhand.) He watched the better players carefully, analyzing their strokes, their footwork, their technique, and then copying them later by himself, playing against the wall. He learned from the movements of the highly regarded, left-handed player Don Nelson Uraga, who had the tenacious fighting spirit that Pancho admired. He practiced his grip, his footwork, his positioning. He worked on the abandoned old rackets at his disposal as though they were priceless—binding the disintegrating strings with tape to make them last longer.

He began to improve his game. "By playing against the wall all the time I knew the ball came back fast, and I learned to hit the ball early." Born with instincts and coordination, in spite of his physical disadvantages, Pancho began to develop compensatory reflexes. He also started working out on a rowing machine, a new addition to the club. His godfather, J. J. Medina, saw to it that his godchild was smuggled into the hallowed exercise room when nobody else was around. By about the age of eleven, the relentless practice, the intense concentration, and the focused mind of the unlikely athlete started to pay dividends. He acquired a proper racket, a well-worn Top Flight, abandoned at the club by a visiting Brazilian. "He looked at it with pride," recalled his mother, "as if it were a treasure, and he used it for many years."

People began to take notice. "Soon," Pancho said with a glint in his eye, "I began beating the big boys." Working at the club, he would sometimes be invited by members to hit with them. Not that they saw it as competition exactly—who would think of a serious matchup between the experienced adult and the puny *pata de loro*, or "parrot foot," as he was called. He didn't even wear proper shoes or socks. But he could hit the ball like the devil, and his consistency made him almost like the ball machines that later dominated tennis coaching. If nobody was around to play at the club, and no pro was available, the members would call on the skinny *cholo*. "I was a ball hitter for them and they would pay me thirty cents, fifty cents, to play with them."

Fifty cents doesn't sound like much, but for Pancho and his family it was a small fortune. His parents' struggle to provide for such a large brood remained a constant anxiety, particularly for his mother, who often could not pay the bills. His father's attitude toward money was more pragmatic. "Don't go out in the rain, we have no raincoats," was the kind of advice he offered his children. Or, "If you must buy a suit, buy a black one that you can wear to wakes and get free food." For their unpromising son to bring home money, however little it was, was a lifesaver.

To discover that tennis was a way to provide funds for the family was a revelation that transformed Pancho's thinking about his life and his future. "Playing tennis brought money to the house, and so my parents encouraged it," he said, recognizing the immense implications of his gift.

He worked harder on his game, and soon the club members could not help but be aware of this determined youngster always hanging around the courts. By playing with the big boys, Pancho developed his game and learned from them, revealing an intense competitiveness that surprised his opponents. Soon, as well as being their ball boy, he also became their regular hitter, making small sums of money each time. "But they never paid up!" he remembered, laughing. "I would wait outside while they changed and then ask for my thirty cents!" This was Pancho's first exposure to the thoughtlessness of the wealthy, who would demand his time and his talent and then walk away. Later, when he began his journey through the glamorous tennis world of the rich and famous, he was to understand this callous habit only too well, and, just as he did as a teenager at the Guayaquil Tennis Club, he would shrug and offer a resigned smile at the irony of it all.

In 1935, when Pancho was thirteen, an important visitor came to the club. He was Francisco Rodriguez Garzon, a well-known journalist and editor of the sports section of the local daily newspaper, *El Telegrafo*. He saw Pancho play, and a few days later, the newspaper published a story about him that caused a minor sensation. "As soon as I saw him," Rodriguez wrote,

that young, simple, shy boy, who became even more nervous when I told him to allow himself to be photographed, he entered deep in my soul. He was afraid that the *señores* would get upset and he did not want to say much of his passion for tennis, of his abilities, and of what he can do. But upon talking to the members of the tennis club I have begun thinking about what a young man . . . with such a familiarity of the racket, of the ball, of the secrets of tennis, and with the ability to impress the whole country with his talents, can achieve.

Thus began a lifelong love affair between *El Telegrafo* and its new young star. This article also announced to the world for the first time that Guayaquil had somebody in their midst who might one day become a national hero. The members of the Guayaquil Tennis Club could no longer ignore the little *mestizo* who had been their ball boy for so long. Pancho began to beat their best players on a regular basis. "They did not always like it," he grinned. "They would call 'foul!'"

On one occasion a well-known North American player known as Mr. Brown came to play at the club. He had heard about the ball boy with the remarkable flair for tennis and was intrigued enough to ask the club if he might play the kid. The club officials reluctantly agreed. Pancho won the match in three sets with ease. Far from being annoyed at this insult from a *cholo* ball boy, the visiting *gringo* was very impressed, told the club they had a seriously gifted player on their hands, and urged them to stop employing him as a ball boy and allow him the opportunity to make a career out of tennis. "This boy, when he is seventeen, will shine, and will make his country shine."

But while some of the club members still found it difficult to accept that the little Indian might be a serious contender as a tennis player, one family in particular began to take an interest in this exceptional talent in their midst. In 1937, Luis Eduardo Bruckmann Burton and his wife, Angela, decided to take personal charge of the club's unlikely prodigy. They invited Pancho to spend time with them in their summer house in Quito. They did not know then that he would become a great player, but they had heard the stories and understood that they could help him by taking care of him for a while.

Quito, the capital of Ecuador, is a beautiful city situated high up in the mountains, where the air is much better and clearer than in Guayaquil, and where those who can afford it prefer to spend the less attractive months of the year. The Bruckmann Burtons offered Pancho a generous deal. They would feed him nourishing food, see that he had proper sleep, and allow him to breathe good air in a healthy environment. In return, he would teach tennis to their two teenage daughters, Ilse and Olga. It was a splendid opportunity, and Pancho seized it with gratitude. The Bruckmann Burtons kept their promise. In Quito, he ate well, became stronger, exercised his growing limbs, adding muscle and tone. As for the rest, he spent a delightful time with Ilse and Olga, who, as he pointed out later, were both extremely pretty.

Pancho spent two months with the Bruckmann Burton family in Quito, and returned in far better shape than when he had left. He was now sixteen years old, and his first big test as a tennis player was about to take place.

Chapter Two

The Education of a Tennis Prodigy

P ancho returned home from Quito in the spring of 1938. He had been three months away from home, in the cool high altitude, playing tennis every day. When he appeared at the Guayaquil Tennis Club for the first time after his absence, it was clear he was transformed. Stronger, faster, fitter, he was playing brilliant tennis. He was also extremely competitive. When he played with the members, he played to win.

The club players were impressed. Some of them also realized their little Pancho could be of immense use to them. Coming up was the annual tennis tournament between Guayaquil and Quito. The two major cities in Ecuador historically enjoyed an intense political rivalry, and the tennis tournament was no different. It was a fiercely fought match that represented the most important championship in the country. This year a group of members of the Guayaquil Tennis Club decided they should invite Pancho to participate in the tournament.

Pancho Segura? Play for the Guayaquil Tennis Club? A lot of people were outraged at the suggestion. The little *cholo*, the ball boy? He wasn't a member, could never in a million years become a member. The idea was ridiculous. How could this poor caretaker's son represent the cream of Guayaquil in such a socially important sporting event? Moreover, he was professional, wasn't he? Hadn't he taken money to play with the members over the years? So what if it was only fifty cents? The club could not countenance any threat to its amateur status. The outcry was loud and persistent.

This was the first time Pancho experienced the reality of his position. He had innocently knocked on the door of a world that would never forget where he came from. At the age of sixteen, he was discovering how many obstacles there were for him to face if he continued his career in tennis, not only physical and mental but social. The physical and mental barriers he had already proved he could negotiate successfully; the social ones presented a more intangible and complex threat.

It took some cunning maneuvering to solve the problem of getting Pancho to Quito. There was no way he could represent the Guayaquil Tennis Club. He wasn't a member and never could be a member. That was that. But his supporters found a way around this ruling by having the young player represent another club in town, which was happy to sponsor him in the tournament.

So Pancho Segura went to Quito. Thrilling, yes. It was his first major appearance on the national tennis circuit, a moment he had been working toward for years. But he was made to pay a painful price for his acceptance. His teammates were not at all pleased at being told to play with this social upstart, and they expressed themselves in the subtle and not-so-subtle ways of class superiority. Pancho may have been part of the team, but he was absolutely not a member of the club. They would not let him sit with them on the train trip to Quito, forcing him to travel by himself in a third-class compartment. He was not allowed to eat with them, either. The club players went out for pork chops, leaving him behind. Since, unlike them, he had no money, he was reduced to buying plantain chips from a street vendor.

Pancho accepted this treatment without bitterness. His job was to play tennis for Guayaquil, and with typical focus, he responded fervently to the challenge. He won all three of his matches, contributing to Guayaquil's defeat of their longtime rival. "We beat the hell out of them," Pancho observed with a satisfied grin. On the way home, his teammates were more respectful of the little *cholo* ball boy. He could win matches for them, it appeared. On the train back to Guayaquil, he was allowed to sit with the rest of the group.

After this triumph, Pancho was no longer an unknown player.

Many people had watched him play in Quito, and they were not about to forget him. The speed! The anticipation! The unheard-of, two-handed forehand! Spectators were astonished at this phenomenon. One man in particular was startled by the talent shown by the dark little teenager from Guayaquil. He was Galo Plaza Lasso, president of the Ecuador Olympic Committee (he later became president of Ecuador). Plaza had been educated at Georgetown University in the United States and was an imposing, fair-haired man of considerable elegance. He decided to invite Pancho to join the Ecuador tennis team entering in the Bolivarian Olympics in Bogotá later that year.

Once more, there was resistance. Peru, a participating country, again brought up the issue of Pancho's professional status, and again, his supporters scoffed at the allegation. Plaza went so far as to threaten to boycott the games if Pancho were banned. The Peruvians withdrew their objection, and Pancho was accepted as part of the Ecuador delegation.

By this time, the people of Guayaquil knew that they had a new popular hero. "The day he left," his mother said, "he was seen off by a musical band. As we, all of his family and friends, took a bus from the Cuba neighborhood, we banged on the car, making a lot of noise and cheering Pancho on." Her pride in her son was almost palpable. This was by far the biggest thing that had happened to her family, and she could only wave, weep, cheer, and pray for him.

Tennis pundits believed that Venezuela and Colombia were the favorites to win the medal, with Peru a close third. But a few spies had heard about the little Ecuadorian sensation and were openly saying that Pancho Segura was the man to beat. Right from the start of the games, this seemed to be the case. Segura's first match was against the Colombian Gastón Moscoso. Although heckled by the crowd who called him a "professional champion," Pancho ignored the distractions and beat Moscoso in three easy sets. The Ecuadorian then faced the Peruvian champion, Carlos Acuna y Rey, and beat him even more easily. Acuna was furious at being defeated by this little nobody and refused to be photographed with him after the match. In the semifinals, Pancho rolled to yet another three-set win against the Bolivian champion Gastón Zamora.

On August 13, 1938, to everyone's astonishment, the gold medal final was between Pancho Segura of Ecuador and Jorge Combariza of Colombia. By this time, the whole of the tournament was in an uproar. Pancho's style of playing, his two-handed forehand, his speed, his spirit, were the talk of the games. The buzz was intense. All the players and fans wanted to see for themselves this completely new kind of tennis played by an unknown player from a small town in Ecuador. Crowds poured on to the court to see this phenomenon play. Tickets were scarce, if not impossible. Back home, *El Telegrafo* promised to transmit the game through Radio Nueva Granada. People in Guayaquil poured into the streets, waiting to hear about the triumph of their beloved prodigy.

Combariza was the favorite and received cheers from his supporters as he appeared on the court. Pancho followed him to polite applause. The contrast was striking—the athletic-looking Colombian with his wealthy entourage, striding grandly on to the court like a pasha, and little Segura, just eighteen years old and weighing 120 pounds, darting quickly to his side of the net, eager to begin. Combariza served first. Pancho seemed nervous and lost five games in a row. The Ecuadorian fans in the bleachers started to urge him on with encouraging cheers, and he responded by winning the next five games. But the price for that courageous comeback was too great, and he lost the first set 7–5.

Pancho began to find his form in the second set, and won it 6–4. By then, the little Indian was "in the zone," as he would say later. His shot-making became more precise, his speed more daunting, his overheads immaculate, his baseline drives like bullets, his volleying faultless. "I was too quick for him," Pancho said later. "I was at the net before the ball had landed on the other side." Combariza had no chance against this tireless whirlwind and lost the last two sets by the humiliating score of 6–1, 6–1.

The spectators rushed down from the stands to congratulate the unexpected champion, and his delirious teammates hoisted him up on their shoulders and marched him in a victory parade round the court. *El Telegrafo* published an AP report that said, in part, "Critics who went to the singles finals all agree that the encounter between Francisco Segura and Jorge Combariza was the best match they saw in Bogotá. They also affirm that Segura exhibited the best tennis of all those observed throughout the tournament."

But the Guayaquileños had to wait to celebrate. The Radio Nueva broadcast never came through, and the news was ultimately transmitted by phone from Rodriguez to the local firemen. As their sirens began to reverberate throughout the city (for once not warning about a fire), everyone started shouting and cheering and jumping up and down that their "favored son, in this hour of triumph . . . had snatched another shred of glory for his beloved Ecuador," as *El Telegrafo* put it in its most patriotic language.

Segura was eighteen years old. His rise had been meteoric. From a humble ball boy hitting for the club members in Guayaquil, he was now not only an internationally known tennis player but the national champion. His return home to Guayaquil was that of a hero. People flocked into the streets in droves to welcome him. A ticker-tape parade was organized. Kids shouted his name as he walked in the streets, travelers on the buses stuck their heads out of windows to salute him. "Everyone invited me into their homes," Pancho remembered. "The delegation gave me a big welcome. I got medals, banners in my honor, everything!" A street was named in his honor. It was only after this triumphal recognition that the belated decision was made to accept him as a member of the Guayaquil Tennis Club.

During 1939, Pancho Segura represented Ecuador in four major South American championships—in Uruguay, Chile, Brazil, and Argentina. He won all of these tournaments. Perhaps his biggest victory was at Millington Drake Stadium, in Carrasco, near Montevideo, against the Argentine champion Lucilo Del Castillo.

Most fans had not yet seen the notorious double-handed tennis player from Ecuador, with the wicked ground strokes and exceptional speed. Anticipation ran high, and as play progressed it was soon clear that Del Castillo was being seriously challenged. At one set apiece, Del Castillo had a set point, which Segura negated and went on to win 11–9. This long set victory was the turning point. There was no more hope for Del Castillo after that. Pancho won the match in four sets.

There was still one more match to play. It was for the tournament cup, played in the presence of the British ambassador, Sir Eugen Millington Drake, for whom the Carrasco stadium was named. Sir Eugen was a great tennis enthusiast and headed the Uruguayan Tennis Federation that had initiated the tournament. The ambassador shook Pancho's hand warmly as he entered the stadium, perhaps aware of the significance of the contest ahead. Pancho's opponent was the Uruguayan champion Sebastien Harreguy, playing here on his home turf. This gave him an immediate advantage, and the crowd roared its support for him as the players walked on to the court.

On this tense occasion, Pancho found it more difficult than usual to read the other man's game. After winning the first set 7–5, he lost the second and third 1–6, 0–6, humiliating scores that he had not racked up throughout the year so far. The crowd began to mutter and murmur, wondering whether to write him off as a one-day wonder after all. But under this intense pressure, Pancho showed the spirit and tenacity that were to become the hallmarks of his style. Like all great players, he found a way to raise the level of his game, and by picking up speed and driving his shots with more power and accuracy, he won the fourth set 6–1. This unsettled the Uruguayan and his fans, who had tasted victory. Harreguy showed signs of fatigue at the start of the fifth set and temporarily left the court with leg cramps. The delay failed to restore him, and he lost the final set 6–3. Sir Eugen Millington Drake, appreciating the fine tennis he had witnessed, presented Segura with the trophy.

This time the response was unanimous. Francisco Segura was a tennis player for the ages. Even his opponents graciously recognized his talents and potential. Millington Drake, inspired to literary heights by his appreciation of the fine match, described the story of the tournament as the twilight of the gods of classical tennis, Del Castillo and Harreguy, both of whom now found themselves in the shadow of Segura, the new shining star.

From this championship Pancho went on to others, in Chile, Brazil, and Argentina again. Each time he returned home his name was bigger. His image was everywhere, always the wiry, dark-skinned young man holding his tennis racket in both hands, his face illuminated by a wide, infectious grin that even then was beginning to melt girls' hearts.

The press wouldn't leave him alone. *El Telegrafo* now routinely called him a Greek god, deserving of hosannas and victory wreaths. "Segura has been the youthful exponent of our people, who has shown our brother nations the vigor of our race, the unbreakable strength of its will . . . its dignity, its discipline, and courage." This nationalistic language was in part an effort to give hope to the poor and disenfranchised masses of this small, struggling country, whose sufferings might perhaps be forgotten in the temporary glory of one of their popular heroes. He belonged to the people—that was the important fact. He was a *criollo* (a commoner), not a *señor* (a patrician), and his victories gave hope to thousands of those sharing the poverty that he had endured.

In fact, the situation was deeply ironic, for becoming a national hero meant nothing in financial terms. Winning tournaments did not translate into economic success. Although his parents had begun to enjoy the enormous public acclaim their eldest son was receiving, their incomes did not change, and the same old difficulties still haunted them as they continued to look for ways to bring up their large family. "My parents began to think they were aristocrats," Pancho said. "They were made such a fuss of. But my success didn't bring in any money."

Ticker-tape parades were exciting, but they did not pay the

bills. Only after newspapers and friends picked up the story of the Segura Cano family's continued poverty did the municipality of Guayaquil respond and give them a piece of land on which to build a house. It was on the corner of Cuenca and Quito streets. The building contained a ground-floor shop to bring in rent, and a modest upstairs apartment with four very small bedrooms, a living-dining space, and a tiny kitchen. It was hardly big enough for such a large family, but at least it was theirs, and members of Pancho's family still live there. It was home, even if it was small and inconveniently located. Still unable to afford transport, Pancho had to make a twenty-minute walk every day to and from the tennis club.

From time to time, Pancho's rich friends at the club slipped him money, clothes, supplies. On one occasion while playing abroad, Agustin Febres Cordero, his old supporter, friend, and former president of the club, gave him five hundred dollars to send to his mother. But other influential friends had greater ambitions for their gifted native son. Galo Plaza, his old patron, was now president of Ecuador. Continuing his interest in the local hero, he suggested that Pancho go to study tennis in France. France was one of the foremost tennis-playing countries in the world, along with Great Britain, Australia, and the United States. Plaza thought France would be an easier place for the inexperienced, poorly educated young South American to feel at home in than the cutthroat competitive world of the United States. In France he would have the opportunity to refine his game and become an international star for Ecuador, indeed, put Ecuador on the map in the most spectacular fashion. No other Ecuadorian athlete to that point had come close to Pancho's international success, and Ecuador was prepared to sponsor their young prize by giving him an allowance to live abroad.

But the world had other plans. Pancho was playing in a tournament in Argentina when war broke out in Europe. "I saw German warships in the harbor in Buenos Aires," Pancho said. "I knew what that meant." It was now impossible for him to go to France to play tennis. ("It was the greatest break of my life," he declared later.) In spite of this setback, again fortune shone on him. His fame had spread and was to reach the shores of a country he had only dreamed about.

Elwood Cooke was one of the top amateur tennis players in the United States. In 1939 he had lost in the finals at Wimbledon to Bobby Riggs (who was his partner that same year in their title-winning doubles.) Cooke had read in an English version of New York's Spanish-language newspaper *La Prensa* about the young sensation from Ecuador, Francisco Segura, and when he made a visit to Guayaquil in the spring of 1940, on a goodwill mission with Wilson Sporting Goods, he asked to see the little champion. What he thought is not recorded, but in June 1940, Pancho Segura, with the support of Elwood Cooke, Wilson Sporting Goods, and a promised monthly stipend of one hundred dollars from the Guayaquil Tennis Club, set off for the United States of America as a "special representative of the Sports Ministry." The arrangement was to last for one year.

"A tender silence of sadness and tears is spreading step by step and from corner to corner," sighed Ralph Del Camp, the poetically inspired writer for *El Telegrafo*, describing the people's grief at Pancho's departure. "Let us remember how upon crossing a sidewalk a small child watched you and uttered in a strangled voice (*con voz en cuello*), 'There goes Pancho Segura, champion of champions.'" Words of advice followed. "Pancho, the chance that you most desired has come. You go to the city of skyscrapers and clamorous noise. But I remind you of this: do not change anything, even if they offer you the National Bank. Be the modest and simple young man that I met, the friend of all."

What did his poor mother think? "*Mama*," Pancho told her one day, "they have given me a grant, but I think I will not use it. I am sure that you will not let me go. *Verdad, mamita?*" But Francisca Cano Segura was made of sterner stuff. "I was a little sad because my son was leaving me," she conceded later, "but I saw the reality of things and I told him, 'But son, why do you think that I won't let you go? Of course I want you to go, so that you will get to know . . . and understand what life is (*de lo que es la vida*).'"

With the last farewells completed, Pancho Segura was ready. He sailed on a Grace Line ship, one of those huge white steamers he had gazed at so longingly from a distance as a child. Now at last, his yearning was a reality. Accompanied by Juan Aguirre, another tennis player from Guayaquil, he was finally on board one of the magnificent vessels of his dreams.

The sea voyage was thrilling to the novice traveler, particularly crossing the Panama Canal. He was enthralled by the miracle of engineering that created it—to be able so quickly to cross from one continent to the other. Throughout the long journey, Pancho had a wild and wonderful time. He used to spend hours in the ship's nightclub, where the performers were singing one of the biggest popular hits of 1940:

> Oh, Johnny, Oh, Johnny, how you can love!
> Oh, Johnny, Oh Johnny, Heavens above!
> You make my sad heart jump for joy,
> And when you're near me
> I can't keep still a minute
> Because it's Oh Johnny, Oh Johnny,
> I love you so!

Pancho would listen, loving it, learning it by heart. "But of course I didn't understand a word!"

The young Ecuadorian was free for the first time from the restraints of his home life and the culture of his country, and he could hardly contain his delight. "There was a girl on the boat who liked me a little bit, but I couldn't speak English so I couldn't make any moves!"

He was traveling to a strange country, where he didn't know a soul. He had no money. He faced an unknown future, speaking not a word of English. But for the eager *cholo* from Guayaquil, this was one of the most exciting moments of his life.

Galo Plaza Lasso had feared that the United States would be too tough for the little Ecuadorian prodigy to make a name for himself playing tennis. But Pancho had other plans, and now there was no turning back.

Chapter Three *Hasta Luego!*

On July 29, 1940, Pancho Segura arrived in New York City. He wore a card with his name on it round his neck, like an immigrant just off the boat. Elwood Cooke and his tennis-playing wife, Sarah, met him at the pier with a representative of Wilson Sporting Goods, and without any more ado, they put him on a train for Southampton, Long Island. He was told he was going to the Meadow Club to play tennis.

Perhaps it was a blessing that at that time Pancho spoke no English. He had no idea that he was about to cross the threshold of one of the most exclusive private clubs in the United States. He had no idea that there were rules of clothing and deportment that the club members most definitely required. He had no idea of his most glaring deficiencies—that he was not white, rich, or college educated.

The Meadow Club had never seen anything like it.

Clutching his shabby tennis racket and a small bag of unsuitable clothes, he arrived in Southampton in time to play in the men's doubles (with his traveling companion, Juan Aguirre), in the Fifteenth Annual Tournament of the Meadow Club.

It was a rout. They lost at once in straight sets, 6–1, 6–2.

Friends put it down to the long journey, to nerves, to the alien environment. But the loss was more simply explained. The match was played on grass, and Pancho had never played on grass in his life. ("Grass? I thought it was something you smoked," he joked later.) These days, players know precisely how to adjust their game from cement or clay to the much faster, quirky surface of grass. Segura and Aguirre had no idea what was happening to their game. Faced with low, fast, skidding balls, they could not adjust their footwork, they could not anticipate, they lost their timing. "My opponent hit a kicker and I missed and people thought I had done it deliberately!" Their tennis looked amateurish in the face of their more skilled opponents. (Pancho also lost a singles match during that tournament.)

But the experience was not a total disaster. Although he lost his matches, audiences could not help noticing the five-foot-six, leather-dark dynamo with his curly jet-black hair, crooked legs, and astonishing double-handed forehand. "Nobody had ever seen anyone play with two hands," Pancho said. "They thought it was all wrong!" Right from the start, the odd-looking player, with his huge grin, had an exotic quality that people found intriguing. They sensed his speed, his energy, his gamesmanship.

One day, as Pancho was making his way back to town on foot from the Meadow Club (of course he had no car), the player who won the Southampton singles championship that year drove by and, seeing the solitary little figure with his odd gait walking along the road, stopped and gave him a ride. The driver's name was Bobby Riggs. Riggs had no idea who the dark-skinned kid was, and Pancho could not speak English, so not much was said on that occasion. But from that moment on, Segura and Riggs struck up a friendship that was to greatly enliven the history of American tennis. They became two of the most popular players on the tour and remained friendly rivals and gambling companions throughout their lives.

A young teenager also paid particular attention to this unlikely new arrival. She was Rosalind Palmer, a young member of the club who had been appointed as Junior Hostess for the weekend, to act as escort for the visiting players. She had been assigned to the young South American while he played in the tournament.

He could not have had better luck in his life.

Rosalind Palmer was fifteen years old. Her father was chairman of the board of E. R. Squibb, and her mother was a poet and playwright, with a graduate degree from Columbia University, who had served as a nurse during World War I. Mrs. Palmer was also a New Deal Democrat who worked with Eleanor Roosevelt in the 1930s and was extremely left-wing in her politics. With such an unconventional background, Rosalind was the product of a stimulating socialist childhood. Later, she got into Smith College, but America had entered the European war, and her mother decided she would do better doing war work. Rosalind got a job in an aircraft plant and gained immortality as the model for Rosie the Riveter.

Considering the type of Meadow Club member who might have been selected as Pancho's "greeter," Rosalind could hardly have been a more brilliant choice to welcome to America a colored *cholo* from a country riddled with class hierarchies and devastating poverty. Oblivious to the obvious shock value of this little dark-skinned imp mingling with the tall, stylish WASP members of the tennis establishment, she took to her scandalous assignment with enthusiasm.

"I watched him play," she remembered. "And I saw his flashing smile. It didn't matter to me if he lost. He made a great impression."

Rosalind Palmer was smitten. So she spoke no Spanish and he spoke no English. Who cared? She understood him perfectly. They got along right from the start. She accompanied him to the courts and to dinners for the players on Friday and Saturday night. After she went home to her parents, Pancho slept in the locker room. He didn't mind. He was nineteen years old, he was in America, he was playing tennis, and he was being looked after by a lovely young girl. What a delightful introduction to the New World!

It was the beginning of a lifelong friendship, one of many that Segura, with his extraordinary talent for finding and keeping friends, found more and more precious over the years. The feeling was mutual. Decades later, Rosalind would express the same feeling of warmth and affection for the little Indian that she had experienced when she first met him at the Meadow Club so long ago.

The week after the Southampton tournament, Pancho was sent

to East Orange, New Jersey, for the Eastern Clay Court Championships. On this occasion he felt a little more comfortable—clay, after all, was a surface he knew well. "I loved clay," he explained, "because I had a good drop shot and drop shots are very effective on clay." Pancho worked out a good strategy on the slower surface. "I would look as though I was hitting it low, my opponent would think I'm going to hit a long drive, and at the last minute I would turn my wrist and produce a drop shot. Good fake!"

This cunning play worked very effectively in one of the most important matches he played in the tournament. It was against Jack Kramer, who was to become a key figure in Pancho's career. Kramer, who was only nineteen, the same age as Pancho, had already won the National Boys' Championship, moved on to the Davis Cup and had beaten most of the top players in the country. Later that year he won the U.S. Nationals in men's doubles. His experience far exceeded that of the little Ecuadorian, he was already famous for his big serve, and it seemed it would be an easy match.

But as Kramer later recalled, "Pancho sort of knocked me off the court in the first set. I was trying to find his weaker shot, which was his backhand, a rather mediocre slice at that time. But it was very hard to get to that shot because Pancho was so quick and he anticipated so well that almost no matter where you hit the ball, he was able to get around it and hit his favorite shot, the two-hander." Kramer went on to say that this was also Pancho's undoing in those days, since he wore himself out running extra steps all the time trying to get to his lethal forehand. "I think he beat me 6–love in the first set, and then I was able to slow him down a little and finally beat him."

In spite of increasing recognition of his talent by other players, Pancho was still coming up with losing scores. His first major assignment on grass after the embarrassing showing in Southampton was at Forest Hills, then the center of U.S. tennis. He was slated to play Frank Parker in the first round on September 4, 1940. It was a tough draw. Frank Parker at this time had been playing Davis Cup since 1937, and was to go on to win two U.S. singles titles in 1944 and 1945, as well as being a finalist in 1942. He knew the grass surface well and was a clever strategist. Tennis writer Eugene L. Scott called him perhaps "the most unsung American hero in tennis of his time." This was to be Pancho's first opponent on grass after the Ecuadorian's humiliating debut in Southampton.

It is to Pancho's great credit that even in those few short weeks, he had already begun to examine the question of playing on grass. He had little opportunity to practice, since he didn't know anybody and had no money, but when he faced Frank Parker he did not disgrace himself. The score was 6–3, 6–1, 7–5 in favor of the more experienced player, a very respectable performance. The plucky last set in particular, when Pancho began to show off to best advantage his crushing two-handed forehand, precision ground strokes, and irresistible tenacity, created a wave of interest and sympathy amongst the spectators, who cheered him warmly at the end.

In October 1940, he won his first grass-court victory in the United States. In a tournament organized by the Hispanic Tennis Club, he beat the Irish champion and Davis Cup player George Lyttleton 6–2, 6–4. Segura's fast-improving tennis now showed a repertoire of devastating shots—deep crosscourt drives, smashes, and drop shots, and of course the vicious two-handed forehand. As Manuel Laverde, tennis writer for *La Prensa*, wrote: "Rogers could not conceal his astonishment each time Segura gave him his celebrated two-handed stroke (*guantón*) that left the Irishman standing at the baseline." Pancho was beginning to get the measure of this strange new green surface and was turning it to his advantage.

But if his tennis was improving, his living conditions were not. Originally it had been arranged for Segura to stay with the Ecuadorian consul in New York, Sixto Durán Ballén. But because of Segura's early losses, the government of Ecuador began getting cold feet about supporting their "special representative." What kind of representative was he if he got trounced almost every time he appeared on an American tennis court? The allowance he had been promised mysteriously dried up.

Winter was coming. There would be fewer and fewer opportunities to practice tennis, the one thing Pancho knew he must do if he was to make any headway in this new country. He was cold, lonely, and practically penniless. On one occasion he came back to a temporary apartment to find his clothes on the sidewalk, because he could not pay the rent. He later told a friend about these terrible days, describing them in his typically racy language, "They left me screwed in New York and I didn't even speak English!"

At this difficult time, he met a Spanish-speaking writer who covered tennis for *La Prensa*. He took pity on the unhappy Ecuadorian and introduced him to a Puerto Rican family in Spanish Harlem. The family took him in. Segura knew his first task was to learn English, so he found a school in the area that offered Spanish lessons. "I made a mistake," he laughed. "It turned out to be a Portuguese Jewish synagogue." He learned English anyway, picked up odd jobs working as a waiter, and often made desperate trips to the Ecuadorian consulate for money. At Christmas they generously gave him twenty dollars.

It was a miserable winter. He wrote pleading letters to the Ecuadorian government, begging for his stipend. He asked if he might be granted a scholarship to a college in California, where he knew he would be able to play tennis on a regular basis. The Ecuadorian authorities sent him small sums from time to time, citing resolutions and conflicting commitments that prevented them from sending any more. The situation was dire. He felt like the lowest form of immigrant.

He would walk to Horn and Hardart (about forty blocks) to get a cheap sandwich. The walk made him feel good, for he was worried about conditioning as the winter months progressed. "Then I'd go to Forty-second Street and see burlesque. 'Take it off! Take it off!' I would shout with the other guys, not knowing what it meant! They were such gorgeous blondes. I thought all Americans were blonde. I didn't know there was such a thing as peroxide."

He was desperately lonely. He had come from a large family, and he missed his sisters and brothers back in Guayaquil. He wrote to his mother once a week until he could no longer afford to do so. He couldn't go anywhere except on foot, because transportation cost too much. He managed once to get to Radio City Music Hall and saw the dancing girls. "Big excitement!" he recalled. He longed for female company, but couldn't afford a date. "There was a German girl learning English like I was, and I liked her but I didn't have any money. 'Take me to the Statue of Liberty,' she said, and we did, but it never went anywhere. I didn't want to take advantage, not having any money."

Pancho was cold, lonely, and, most painful of all, he could not play tennis. It cost money to rent an indoor court and he had none to spare. Not playing tennis was the one deprivation the hungry and frustrated Ecuadorian could not bear. It was one of the worst periods of his life.

His luck changed in the form of a benefactor whose generosity transported the desolate nineteen-year-old into an entirely new realm. His name was Arturo Cano (no relation), and he was the Bolivian consul to the United States in New York. Cano was charming, witty, and rich. He also loved tennis. He remembered Pancho's triumph at the Bolivarian Games, he knew what the young tennis player was capable of, and he decided to take the skinny kid under his wing. Suddenly, Pancho's fortunes changed radically. Cano lived in a large apartment on Riverside Drive and he invited Pancho to stay with him. "People thought I had money because I lived there," Pancho laughed. Cano took him around town, showed him fine restaurants and nightclubs, such as the Copacabana, the Latin Quarter, and the Diamond Horseshoe. "I didn't always go with him," Pancho said. "I was too young to stay out late. I was always concerned about my fitness."

Cano's influence was enormous. Through him, Pancho met rich people for the first time and saw how they entertained themselves and how he should behave with them. Cano taught him social skills that were invaluable lessons for the boy from the Guayaquil barrio, and they remained with him for life. Pancho was a quick student and knew the value of his good fortune. "He was my patron. I got lucky. He kept me in food and clothes. He was my buddy."

Cano was joined by another South American, Alfonso Rojas, an Ecuadorian newspaper mogul, who also began supporting Pancho, taking care of his correspondence and finances. With these guardians, Pancho now began to experience New York in a completely new way. As well as going to nightclubs and shows with Arturo Cano, he used to see Rosalind Palmer and her parents, who would invite him to dinner and the theater. Rosalind remembered how Pancho would study the posters in the foyer and program notes with a fierce intensity, memorizing the names and faces of actors and actresses. How could he have known that one day he might meet some of them and become their friends?

But tennis came first, and his main desire was to play, wherever and whenever he could. Arturo Cano sensed that his protégé had drawing power on the tennis court, and during the spring and summer of 1941 he entered him in tournaments up and down the East coast. Pancho began playing good tennis. On May 19, 1941, he won his first major tournament, the Brooklyn Tennis Championship. He beat the Czech player Ladislav Hecht in five grueling sets, 3–6, 4–6, 6–1, 6–1, 6–2.

The highly regarded tennis writer for the *New York Times* Allison Danzig covered the match. Clearly bowled over by the extraordinary tennis he had witnessed, he wrote, "No one would have given very much for the chances of the nineteen-year-old South American as the play went into the third set." But as it progressed, "the little fellow from South America never flagged in his concentration and fight." In the fourth set, "Segura, in full control, and gaining in confidence, was too strong from the back of the court, and passed Hecht as the latter came in on unworthy approach shots." Toward the end of the fifth set, "Segura, playing brilliantly and scoring with his two-hand drive and passing shots, ran four games in a row to end the match."

Danzig added that the Ecuadorian received an ovation from his friends in the big crowd. Arturo Cano had called it correctly—Pancho Segura, the Inca Warrior, was becoming a major tennis draw.

That was the beginning of a great summer for Pancho. He played at all the elite clubs of the Northeastern circuit—Longwood Cricket Club in Brookline, Massachusetts; Seabright Lawn Tennis and Country Club, New Jersey; the Meadow Club in Southampton; the Westchester Country Club in Rye, New York; the Newport Casino, Rhode Island; and finishing at the West Side Country Club in Forest Hills, New York. These were lawn tennis clubs with notorious membership exclusivity. In the face of every kind of odds, the little *morocho* was finding his feet—on the most exclusive lawn tennis courts in the world.

At Forest Hills he was again drawn against Frank Parker, and again he lost. But in his last tournament of that year, in the Dade County Championship in Miami, he beat one of the best players in the country, Gardnar Mulloy, in an upset that astounded the tennis world. The score was 4–6, 6–1, 6–1, 6–4, 8–6. The match was widely reported by the international press, who were dazzled by the speed and tenacity of the little South American marvel, who had seemingly come out of nowhere to defeat Mulloy, the seven-time amateur champion.

Pancho always said that Gardnar Mulloy first saw him play at Forest Hills in 1941, and was so taken by the young outsider's game that he said, "That little Indian can be a great player." Mulloy's memory is different. He said that he first saw Pancho play in Guayaquil before the war, when Mulloy was visiting Ecuador with the State Department.

"When we visited these clubs we would be asked to play with the juniors, and in Guayaquil they dragged out this bandy-legged little kid. I hit with him and he was good. When you hit with a junior you can usually tell within five minutes if he's going to be any good or not. I said to the members of the Guayaquil Tennis

Club that this kid had to get to the United States and if he ever came I'd be glad to help him."

In 1941, Mulloy was playing in the Eastern Grass Court Championships in Rye, New York, with his doubles partner Bill Talbert. They were in their hotel room and late at night there was a knock on the door. "I opened the door and in the dim corridor light was Segura, standing there with a little straw bag. 'I am Francisco Segura,' he said in his almost impenetrable English. 'You say come America, and here I am.'" Mulloy looked at him for a moment and then said, "Come on in, you can sleep on the floor."

Segura had once again been dealt a lucky hand. Gardnar Mulloy was one of the finest all-around players in the world. He was U.S. doubles finalist in 1940 and 1941, with Bill Talbert, and later a finalist in the French and Wimbledon championships. Gene Scott described him as "blessed with effortless grace and athleticism." But he held another title that was far more important to Pancho at that time. Gardnar Mulloy was coach of the University of Miami tennis team, and thanks to his influence, Segura won a scholarship to the University of Miami starting in the fall of 1942. The university administration was cunningly given the impression that Pancho had the required credits from Ecuador to grant him admission. "The president would keep asking, 'Where are the credits?'" Mulloy recalled. "And Pancho would say, 'They're coming next week.' Of course they never came."

Pancho proved worthy of Mulloy's trust. After losing in a nail-biting match to Ted Schroeder (a top-ranked player who won the U.S. singles title in 1942), in the final of the Sugar Bowl in New Orleans in December 1941, the following year Pancho won the East Coast Championship, the Southampton tournament (both on grass), and lost to his future coach, Gardnar Mulloy, in the final of the Inter-American Championship in Havana, Cuba. In 1942 he also won the Sugar Bowl tournament, but perhaps his greatest triumph that year was beating Mulloy in the grass-court championships at Longwood. (Was it perhaps a little tactless to beat his patron and mentor for a second time? On this occasion Mulloy wouldn't speak to him for a week!) At the end of 1942, Segura was ranked fourth-best amateur player in the United States below Ted Schroeder, Frank Parker, and Gardnar Mulloy. Quite a record to carry around for the South American freshman at the University of Miami.

Tennis scholarships were not uncommon at Miami. In 1936, Gardnar Mulloy had recruited the immensely talented Bobby Riggs in the same role, but Riggs, fixated at that time on becoming a champion tennis player, did not take to university life and skipped most of his classes. In his typically brash fashion, Riggs made a proposition to the college president, Dr. Bowman Ashe, that he should simply play tennis in tournaments across the country, publicizing the University of Miami, and at the end be awarded his diploma. Dr. Ashe, not surprisingly, did not buy this idea and Riggs disappeared back home to California after only about a month in school.

Pancho Segura was made of sterner stuff. He knew he had to make his way more carefully. With no money and few contacts, his best bet was to study well, improve his tennis, and keep his head down. The University of Miami gave him food, a roof over his head, and unlimited access to tennis courts run by a brilliant coach. What could be better for him at this stage in his career?

It wasn't easy, of course. His English was still minimal. He was placed in a dormitory with a group of football players. The physical incongruity could hardly have been more extreme; the little Indian bunking up with linemen, defensive ends, and all the other two-hundred-pound, corn-fed athletes playing football for the University of Miami. They threw him around like a rag doll. They teased him unmercifully. "Sissy! What's the game you play? Tennis? What a sissy game!" They played on his poor English.

"See that gorgeous girl over there?"

Pancho would look longingly at her.

"Go over there and say, 'I want to make love to you.' She'll really like you if you say that."

"Really?"

"Sure."

Pancho would go over to the girl and articulate the sentence in his halting English. The result was predictable—a hearty slap in the face.

Pancho didn't mind. It was all valuable exposure for him to American customs, American language, American jokes, clues about the culture he was later able to exploit so brilliantly. "There were only two Spanish-speaking students in a class of 2,500," he said. "I had to learn fast. I used to go to the dining room an hour before the football players got there because otherwise I knew the food would be gone!" His classmates were mostly rich. "They all had cars. I used to take a bus to the city of Miami. I had a good friend who loved tennis, and he would drive me around or lend me his car. He was on the tennis team and I beat him all the time."

Pancho was there for the tennis, but he embraced the rest of his university career eagerly and began to exercise an intelligence that went far beyond tennis strategy. He applied for classes he thought he might have a chance of passing, including forestry and business administration. (Mulloy used to tease him later by saying he majored in underwater basket weaving and Spanish.) But the subjects he liked best were politics, current affairs, and history. "I liked listening to the class discussions. I learned a lot by listening. I sat next to the most unattractive girls. They were always the brightest and got the awards. I thought if I sat next to them their knowledge would rub off on me. I had that in mind, you know. The pretty ones were always talking about themselves and who they were going out with."

Not that pretty girls weren't interesting to him. "I had a blonde girlfriend. I tried to put a play on her, but I had no wheels and no money. I couldn't take a girl to a bar even. You can't be a player without wheels. I couldn't even use the drive-in movie! Gorgeous girls! I went to the beach and this girl put cream on my back and I didn't know what to do, I was so nervous!"

Poor Pancho. For him, this was culture shock at its most tantalizing. In South America, women were thought of as saints and virgins, not to be touched until after marriage. The loose, wild sex life of the students he was surrounded by was intoxicating and very frustrating. "In Miami, all those girls, so many, and I just wanted one!"

Gardnar Mulloy was well aware of the pressures on his young recruit. He was coaching Pancho very hard and found him to be a responsive student. "He got better and better." But Mulloy was not about to let him get distracted by other things. "He used to tell me to stay away from girls. He said it's like running five miles!" It's not clear whether Mulloy, who was tall and extremely handsome, took his own advice. Pancho said they used to call him *chupaflor* (hummingbird), "because he likes to suck flowers." Mulloy laughed at that and said, "If I did everything I'm credited for, I wouldn't be able to walk."

Pancho Segura won the NCAA Intercollegiate singles championship for the University of Miami three years in a row, 1943, 1944, and 1945—still a record. In every match he was much smaller and lighter than his opponents. One of them, Tom Brown of Stanford, was considered as good a player as Jack Kramer and became Wimbledon doubles champion with Kramer in 1946. "That was a fantastic win for me," Pancho recalled. "I was like Jimmy Connors or Lleyton Hewitt, 100 percent on every shot, with great concentration. I overcame my handicaps in size and weight. *In my mind I thought I could win.* I showed I had the potential, and that my coach was right to put his trust in me. Mulloy was with me all the way. He told me I would put the school on the map and I did."

Pancho did not graduate—he did not pass enough courses. But he learned more during his university years than he could ever have learned from his professors. Instead of an academic diploma, he earned a degree in a far more useful course—the American Way of Life. By being around these confident young Miami college kids, he saw the promise of America. "I would go to the library and read up on how Americans become rich," he said. Pancho was tasting the possibilities of the American dream—a lesson he was never going to forget. Mulloy used to joke that if it hadn't been for him, Pancho would be climbing coconut trees or checking coats in Ecuador. Pancho knew the truth of this. "If it weren't for tennis," he would say, "I'd be with all the other Indians chasing alligators in Florida's amusement parks."

Gardnar Mulloy continued generously to promote his Indian star and saw to it that he made appearances elsewhere, further enhancing his standing. In January 1943, Pancho won the Pan American Championship in Mexico, and that summer he won the Eastern Grass Court Championship, the Southampton tournament, and an important exhibition match in Miami, where he beat the man then considered the best player in the world, Don Budge.

After Pancho's semifinal win at Southampton's Meadow Club that August, *New York Times* writer Allison Danzig once again showered praise on the surprising Hispanic outsider. Rightly predicting that Segura would win the tournament (in a tough three-set match against the former Wimbledon champion Sidney B. Wood Jr.), Danzig devoted the whole *Sports of the Times* column that weekend to Pancho's career so far. Calling the editorial "Good Neighbor with a Racquet," Danzig described the usual North American attitude to South America as "steel guitars, castanets, the swirling skirts of a Carmen Miranda and polo ponies," and declared that this human dynamo from Guayaquil, Ecuador, "with the best of all freak shots ever seen at Forest Hills, Wimbledon, or St. Cloud," was going to change all that. Danzig went on to say that considering the other top ten names in tennis, "Segura stands as the man to beat."

The column, which dominated the sports pages of the newspaper, is courageous, not only for its daring promotion of a young Latino in the clubby society of amateur tennis, but also for its bold declaration about Pancho's future in the game. "Segura stands as the most colorful figure to pull the crowd into the stadium," Danzig wrote. "The friends he is making with his sportsmanship and good nature, as well as his success on the courts, will bring in plenty for himself in the years ahead." Such lavish and admiring coverage from the top tennis writer at the *New York Times* for a twenty-two-year-old Ecuadorian, who had only been in the United States for three years, is quite a tribute to the Inca Warrior's impact on the world of tennis. (Danzig's column, translated into Spanish, was printed in full the next day in *El Telegrafo*. Guayaquil went wild.)

In 1944, Pancho won the Western Championship and U.S. Clay Court titles. He again won the Southampton tournament, and in 1945, after winning the Pan American tournament again and the U.S. Clay Court doubles championship with Bill Talbert, he retired the Meadow Club cup by winning the Southampton tournament three years in a row. (What better payback for his lackluster debut five years earlier?) At the end of 1945, with his triple win of the Intercollegiate singles for Miami, and having also reached the semis of the U.S. Nationals at Forest Hills three years in a row, Pancho Segura ranked third in the amateur standings behind Frank Parker and Bill Talbert.

While the world war was taking its toll on a larger stage abroad, Pancho criss-crossed the country playing tennis. Because of his legs he was rated 4F and could not be drafted. Instead he played exhibition games at U.S. army and navy bases. He played in any tournament still running, traveling everywhere by Greyhound bus. "I was a vagabond," he said. He went to Nassau in the Bahamas and played for the daughter of the murdered Englishman, Harry Oakes. He played wherever and whenever he could, indoors and outdoors. All the time, he was constantly refining his tennis, particularly on grass. He worked on his net play, on his backhand, and on his serve. He became a ferocious, tireless competitor and the darling of the fans.

But when the war was over, and the great amateur players who had signed up for active service came home, the tennis scene looked very different. In 1946 Pancho won the National Indoor title, the Queen of England's Cup, and the Pan American tournament in Mexico (for the third time). But these were not major Grand Slam titles. The top American players, Don Budge, Jack

Kramer, Ted Schroeder, and Frank Parker, had all quickly returned to big-time tennis, and Segura soon lost his high ranking. The competition was never more fierce.

Pancho's future suddenly looked less promising. Perhaps Danzig's optimism had been misplaced. There was talk about him going home, something he refused even to consider. (He made a brief trip back to Guayaquil in 1945, where he was welcomed like a god, but he did not linger.) He again began to worry desperately about money, and not only for himself this time. The Inca Warrior had fallen in love. But how could he get married?

In late 1947, Jack Harris, the only successful professional tennis promoter in the country, invited Pancho Segura to join his tour. It was the biggest decision of his career.

Chapter Four Love On and Off the Court

At the end of World War II, professional tennis, after a lively start, returned to the dark ages. The game of lawn tennis originated in "real" or court tennis, a complicated racket sport dating from the 1500s, often called the sport of kings. (In Shakespeare's play *Henry V*, the French dauphin sends the English king the insulting gift of tennis balls, provoking Henry to "play a set," that is, launch a battle, that will defeat France.)

Lawn tennis, an adaptation of real tennis played on an outdoor court, was first played in England in 1874, and a year later in the United States. It had originally been introduced to the public in England by Major Walter Clopton Wingfield and soon began to compete in popularity with the other major sport patronized by the leisure classes, croquet. Across the pond, similar enthusiasm was shown for this unusual game, which was played with wood rackets that could be any shape or size, with strings made of gut. In recognition of the growing passion for the newer sport, in 1877 the top London sporting club changed its name to the All England Lawn Tennis and Croquet Club.

Two developments in the late 1800s helped make lawn tennis the success it became. One was the invention of the lawn mower, which could turn large stretches of grass into a firm, even surface, and the other was the introduction of a rubber ball that could bounce on grass, replacing sheepskin-covered balls, which bounced only on stone.

By all accounts, professional tennis started in Europe, when the Czech champion, Karel Kozeluh, and the German, Roman Najuch, started playing for money from 1910 onward, joined on occasion by other, mostly European, players. In 1926, a U.S. pro-

Francisco Segura Cano, aged thirteen, a small ball boy with a big tennis racket. Photo courtesy of Segura family collection.

Pancho Segura, a teenage prodigy, still without proper tennis shoes. Photo courtesy of the Ecuador Olympic Committee.

Pancho, aged twenty-one, with his parents in Ecuador.
Photo courtesy of Segura family collection.

Pancho, aged eighteen, after winning a dramatic four-set match against the
Argentine champion, Lucilo del Castillo, in the South American Championships
in 1939. Photo courtesy of the Ecuador Olympic Committee.

Ecuador's local press hails the country's new tennis champion.
Photo courtesy of the Ecuador Olympic Committee.

Arriving in the United States, Pancho is slated to play seven-time amateur
champion Gardnar Mulloy at a Red Cross benefit at Forest Hills in 1941. Pancho
beats Mulloy in two sets, to the astonishment of the tennis world. (Later that
year Pancho beats him again in four sets at the Dade County Championship in
Miami.) Photo by Max Peter Haas/European Picture Service.

Gardnar Mulloy, coach of the University of Miami tennis team, recognizes the talent of the young Ecuadorian and arranges for him to enroll at the university in 1942. Photo courtesy of the Special Collections, University of Miami Libraries, Coral Gables, Florida.

A whirlwind romance inspired by tennis: Pancho and Long Island beauty, eighteen-year-old Virginia Spencer Smith, in the summer of 1946. Foto Utreras Hermanos, Quito, Ecuador.

Pancho and Virginia at their wedding ceremony in Guayaquil, Ecuador, 1946. Photo courtesy of Segura family collection.

Pancho, Virginia, and their son, Spencer, taking off on a leg of the professional tour in 1960. Photo courtesy of Segura family collection.

At home in Los Angeles in 1960, Pancho and his son, Spencer, keep fit. Photo by Ralph Crane/Time & Life Pictures/Getty Images.

Pancho's unique two-handed forehand, thrilling tennis fans everywhere, becomes his greatest weapon as a player. (*left*) Photo by Arthur Cole/Le Roye Productions. (*below*) Photo by Arthur Cole/Le Roye Productions. (*opposite top*) Photo by Ralph Crane/Time & Life Pictures/Getty Images. (*opposite bottom*) Photo by Ralph Crane/Time & Life Pictures/Getty Images.

Pancho serving and returning
with his trademark bowlegged
stance, physical strength,
and flexibility. (*left*) Photo
by Ralph Crane/Time & Life
Pictures/Getty Images. (*below*)
Photo by Arthur Cole/Le
Roye Productions. (*opposite*)
Photo by Arthur Cole/Le Roye
Productions.

Pancho with Dinny Pails, one of his regular teammates, called by Jack Kramer the "animal act," on the professional tour in the 1950s. Photo courtesy of Segura family collection.

Australian singles and doubles champion Frank Sedgman appears
with Pancho in one of the many brilliant matches the pair played
before delighted fans throughout the world on the pro tour in the
1950s. Photo by Arthur Cole/Le Roye Productions.

(*opposite top*) Jack Kramer (*far right*) with his tour aces in 1948.
Left to right: Bobby Riggs, Don Budge, and Pancho Segura.
Photo courtesy of the Beverly Hills Tennis Club.

(*opposite bottom*) Big Pancho (Richard Gonzales) and Little
Pancho (Pancho Segura) at the Pro Indoor Championships at
Wembley, England, in September 1957. Photo by Arthur Cole/
Le Roye Productions.

(*above*) Pancho with (*from left to right*) Jack Kramer, Frank
Sedgman, and Ken McGregor, in 1952. Photo courtesy of Segura
family collection.

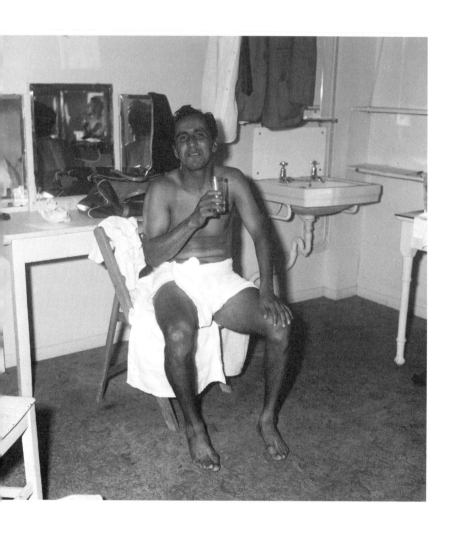

Taking a break after yet another tough match at Wembley in 1956. Photo by Arthur Cole/Le Roye Productions.

moter, Charles C. Pyle, presented a series of matches in which former amateur champions were invited to play professionally for sums of up to thirty thousand dollars. This became the blueprint for the professional tour—the top professional champion would be lined up in a match or series of tournaments in competition against the amateur who had the best record before joining the pro circuit.

The earliest big professional stars were women—the famous Suzanne Lenglen and Mary K. Browne—who drew far better audiences than the men. It is said that Lenglen won one hundred thousand dollars in 1926 before quitting, a sum that the men on the tour, to their chagrin, could not match, and earning her the reputation of femme fatale. It may seem surprising today that women were in the forefront of the moneymakers, but there was good reason. In those early days the feeling among many sports aficionados was that tennis was not really a male thing anyway. Frank Deford writes in his biography of Bill Tilden that tennis "had for so long been associated with effete ladies and gentlemen that it had taken on the image of a sissy game." He adds that Allison Danzig, the tennis writer for the *New York Times*, was originally horrified when he was assigned the tennis beat, a field regarded as a subject for journalistic wimps.

There was another, perhaps more insidious, hostility toward professional tennis in general. According to one of the early pros, Vincent Richards, there was a definite stigma attached to playing for "filthy lucre" as he put it, in those days. "As an amateur tennis star in the twenties, you were showered with hospitality by the social colony. But as a professional you were ignored."

Bill Tilden, who was the greatest amateur champion of his time, encouraged this attitude. On the side, he wrote (rather bad) fiction, and in one short story published in 1924, called "The Amateur," he spells out the distaste he had for professional tennis. One of the characters has to play for money in order to pay his mother's doctor's bills and groans, "God! How he hated the money that was dirtying up the game he loved." Ironically, Tilden himself turned pro in 1930 at the age of thirty-seven.

This resistance to professional tennis was reflected in the fact that there were no professional instructors until 1910. One was supposed to pick up the game from friends and club members, not from an inferior being such as a coach. Bill Tilden himself never took a lesson in his life. (This attitude was to continue; neither Pancho Segura nor Richard Gonzales, two of the greatest players in the history of the game, ever had formal tennis lessons.) As an adolescent Tilden showed only marginal talent and never made the varsity team during his years at the University of Pennsylvania. He learned from practicing, analyzing, and watching others, and in 1920, at the age of twenty-seven, he won the first of his three Wimbledon singles titles.

When Tilden turned pro in 1930, after a series of high-profile wins, his drawing power was such that his tours became highly successful, and during that decade professional tennis became an increasingly credible institution. Names such as Ellsworth Vines (former Wimbledon champion), Frank Hunter (rated in the world's top ten in the late 1920s), Henri Cochet (number one in the world), Vinnie Richards, Hans Nusslein, and Fred Perry helped bring in audiences; Madison Square Garden in New York, Wembley in London, and Roland Garros in Paris became big tourist destinations during the summer tennis season. In 1939 the tour was invigorated by the addition of Don Budge, an attractive crowd-pleaser who a year earlier had been the first tennis player in the world to win the Grand Slam—the Australian, French, Wimbledon, and U.S. singles titles.

The tour's momentum was stopped short by the outbreak of World War II in Europe. No tennis at all to speak of was played in Europe after 1939, and in the United States, the professionals continued as best they could until the country entered the war in 1941. That year two of the most important tennis players in history joined the pros—Bobby Riggs and Frank Kovacs.

Riggs's record was staggering. In 1939 he won all three Wimbledon titles, as well as the U.S. singles, and was runner-up in the French. In 1940 he was a finalist in the U.S. singles, and won the mixed doubles. In 1941, before he turned pro, he won the U.S. singles for the second time and was a finalist in the mixed. Riggs was small and light compared with many of his opponents (in this way he was like Segura), but his strategic skills and speed on the court left most players standing. He was also a compulsive gambler, and the matches (most of which he bet on) became tests of his desire to win as well as of his stamina. Jack Kramer declared that Bobby Riggs was "the most underrated champion in the history of tennis." Sadly, his reputation as a tennis player was totally overshadowed by his later eccentric showmanship, in particular his wildly hyped "Battle of the Sexes" with Billie Jean King in 1973.

Frank Kovacs, a lesser-known but brilliant player, beloved of the fans, also turned pro in 1941. Kovacs was a showman on the court even before Riggs. He was six foot four, with a huge smile, and he would clown around for the audiences. Once he lay down on the tennis court to watch a plane flying overhead. Kovacs brought much-needed humor to the game, just as Pancho Segura did later. Riggs and Kovacs both signed for twenty-five thousand dollars, a respectable sum at that time. These players were significant additions to the pro game, but as America became increasingly involved in the war, tennis naturally took a back seat, and the players abandoned the tour for more patriotic duties.

In 1945, as the war wound down, the World Professional Tennis Association (WPTA) was formed, with plans to hold tournaments every month in a different country. These ambitions were not easily fulfilled, as few pros showed up to play. A tournament under WPTA auspices in the Civic Auditorium in San Francisco, for example, consisted of only four players. In this depleted contest, Kovacs beat Welby Van Horn 14–12, 6–3, to claim the title of "World" Pro Champ.

As more players returned home, they formed a players association under Bill Tilden, hoping to regain their former audiences. But their names were by now old and well-worn, and although during 1946 they played tournaments over eight months across the country, the results were not convincing. A new promoter from

Chicago, Jack Harris, put on a series of matches between Riggs and Budge, the two top draws, which were successful, but on the whole the atmosphere was not encouraging.

As tennis writer Joel Drucker put it, "Pro tennis in those years was similar to baseball's Negro leagues—barred from the major league venues, ostracized by the game's administrators." Distaste for making money out of athletic events continued to give pro tennis a bad name. Added to this, criticisms about match "fixing" constantly swirled around the tour. How could the players continue to maintain a competitive edge when they faced off against each other so often? (This question was to persist until the open tennis era.) Such suspicions dampened audiences' enthusiasm for the tour.

Another more serious blow came with the arrest of Bill Tilden for pedophilia in November 1946. This scandal cast a large shadow on the pro game. Tilden was jailed briefly and then released, but he was later arrested again after being found in his car with a teenage boy. The last years of "the greatest tennis player who ever lived" were desperately sad as the tennis world turned its back on him and he could no longer play the game he loved. Tilden died broke in 1953 in a small rented apartment in Los Angeles, aged sixty. Only a handful of people turned up at the funeral, including big-hearted Pancho Segura.

In 1947, the World Professional Tennis League, formed in yet another effort to promote the game, folded after only nine months of existence because of the lack of champion players. But at this moment of total demoralization, an event took place that changed the future of the professional game. Jack Harris, in a brilliant coup, signed the world's number one amateur player, Jack Kramer, for seventy-five thousand dollars. Kramer was tall, handsome, and a brilliant tennis player, and Harris's vision was to present this golden boy in a series of head-to-head tournaments with the current top pro, Bobby Riggs. At the same time, Harris signed Pancho Segura and the Australian champion Denis "Dinny" Pails, currently ranked sixth in the world, as warm-up players for these two dazzling stars. Thus a new generation of players entered the professional arena, and they dominated the game for the next fifteen years.

For Jack Kramer, who had a wife and four children, turning professional was his only option if he was to make a living playing tennis. But as well as being a marvelous athlete and a good-looker (he was like an all-American movie star on the court), Kramer had a nose for business, and he saw that there was the potential for enormous profits in the pro game. Kramer not only wanted to win his matches but also to make a fortune. This meant taking tennis to the people and making them pay for it. His pro career was entirely dedicated to that goal.

For Segura, the argument for turning pro was simpler. His business plan was simply to make a living doing what he loved. "Harris talked me into becoming a pro," Segura recalled later. "He worked for Wilson Sporting Goods, although nobody knew it at the time, and Wilson actually sponsored the tour. Harris gave me three hundred dollars a week, out of which I had to pay my expenses." Pancho admitted it was a bad deal. "I played for a whole year and made about ten thousand dollars."

But like Kramer, he was in no position to complain. Unbeknownst to his teammates, and also to Jack Harris, Pancho Segura had just gotten married.

Pancho first met Virginia Spencer Smith on the tennis courts at the West Side Tennis Club in Forest Hills during the national championships in 1941. She was thirteen years old. "I was just mingling with the players and discussing the matches and there he was!" she remembered. Entranced by the charming Ecuadorian, she chatted briefly to him and he autographed her *pique* beanie. "And then I went back home."

Virginia was living in Englewood at the time with her parents, going to private school, and learning to play tennis. "My wrist was very flimsy," she admitted. "It would go whoosh! Like this." Hers was a happy life. The Smiths came from old Yankee stock. Her father was in marine insurance and her mother came from a fine

Maryland family, and although there was not much money, they lived well and both adored their beautiful only child.

But then her parents divorced and things changed. Virginia had to leave her large family house in Englewood and her private school. Her mother looked all over for another place to live and finally told her daughter she had reluctantly settled on a small place in Forest Hills. "Forest Hills!" Virginia was delighted. It was her home away from home. "But of course I couldn't join the tennis club right away. Dad had to work something out."

So Virginia went to a new school and went on playing tennis and practically lived at the tennis club. And that's how she saw Pancho again. By this time it was 1946, she was eighteen, and she had spent a year at Endicott Junior College in Boston, studying art and drama. There was a discussion about her spending the summer of 1946 doing summer stock, but it was too expensive, so she lived at the tennis club instead. "There were European tennis players as well as Americans coming and going, nice, young, and cute," she remembered. "And then there was Pancho."

By this time Virginia had turned into a gorgeous young woman, with large azure blue eyes, blonde hair, and a fantastic figure. She was so stunning that she had already been tapped for modeling work. (It was not uncommon in those days for good-looking, well-bred, young ladies to model for the big department stores in New York and Boston.) Pancho was not the kind of man to ignore such a résumé. He focused on her immediately. "We started kidding around," Virginia said, "and he introduced me to Bobby Riggs and told me what an important player he was." Virginia was polite to Bobby Riggs but he was not the person she was interested in. However, Bobby Riggs asked her out. "Come with me," he urged her, "we're going to have a party."

Virginia wasn't sure if Bobby meant in his hotel room, but Pancho at once stepped in and said, "Virginia, don't go there. You'll be sorry." She took the Ecuadorian's advice and didn't go with Bobby Riggs. "So then Pancho became my buddy. He wasn't a boyfriend as we mean it today," she quickly explained. "It was romantic and platonic. It was lovely."

Pancho gave Virginia a whirlwind courtship. He sent her flowers, took her out to the 21 Club and El Morocco. "You must understand," Virginia said, "I had only been out with young boys my age. Pancho was seven years older. In most cases, that would be bad, but he was just so full of fun and very youthful, so age didn't matter."

As for Pancho, he was beside himself. "I was not in love before Virginia. Never. She was the first."

After only a few months he asked her to marry him. Knowing by now the ways of the American WASP, he went to her father to ask for his daughter's hand. Mr. Smith wanted to know if he had any money. "You were supposed to have something," Virginia pointed out, laughing. "And Pancho said, 'Well, I have three thousand dollars!'" Virginia's father, appalled, advised them to wait. But neither Pancho nor Virginia took his advice. Instead they ran off to New York and got married by a judge.

"We had to wait two days so I could be nineteen," Virginia said. "My mother, who, unlike my father, was quite happy to see me married off, arranged for me to stay in a ladies' hotel before the ceremony, so I'd be safe there."

The discovery that the lovely young debutante Virginia Spencer Smith had eloped with a dark-skinned Latino tennis player was a natural for the tabloids, and reporters had a field day with the story. It caused the same kind of disbelief that an earlier coupling had provoked—that of society belle Ellen Mackay eloping with the little Jew, Irving Berlin. Wasn't there something disgraceful about Virginia abandoning her distinguished family roots to throw in her lot with a little Indian tennis player? But while people at home gossiped about the scandal, the wicked couple was long gone—all the way to Ecuador.

For Virginia was not the only one to be in trouble with this shocking marriage. Pancho had his own problems back home. "My mother was very unhappy," Pancho explained. "Virginia wasn't Indian, she wasn't Ecuadorian. Mothers are like that. Mine wanted me to marry one of our own kind. And we hadn't even married in a church." To ease matters, he and Virginia flew to Guayaquil and had a proper formal Ecuadorian marriage in the presence of his family and friends.

The ceremony in the Guayaquil cathedral was organized by one of Pancho's godfathers and patrons, Alfonso Rojas. Virginia found a dressmaker to make her a dress. It was copied from *Vogue*, in blue satin, and it was finished in two days. Everyone from the city turned out to see their national hero, Francisco Segura, marry the stunning blonde *norteamericana*. They mobbed the taxi in which the bridal couple was traveling to the cathedral, rocking it so violently that Virginia was afraid it would topple over.

When they got to the church, the crowds went crazy. Soldiers had to make way for them with bayonets. The most important townspeople walked with them up the aisle and gathered round the altar for the ceremony. Even the president of Ecuador was there.

"Afterward, they prepared a meal for me at Pancho's house," Virginia recalled. "The house was very poor, with holes in the wall. The meal was just for me, in the center of the table. I had to eat it by myself—that was the tradition. They brought me the first course—a mountainous plate of mashed avocados. I thought everyone was watching me through the holes. I could hardly eat but felt I had to finish it."

With the wedding over, Pancho spirited his properly married bride away and returned to real life, which was tennis. The tennis circuit in the summer of 1947 took them to Ecuador, Colombia, Mexico, Argentina, and Brazil. In each place they were wined and dined, greeted by local dignitaries, even ambassadors. "They called us 'coffee and cream,'" Virginia fondly remembered. Everywhere throughout South America they were treated like celebrities. Those whirlwind destinations were the Seguras' honeymoon, and traveling with Pancho that summer was how Virginia learned what it would be like to be married to a husband whose whole life was tennis.

Chapter Five The Professional Circus Act

I t is almost impossible for people today to imagine the kind of life professional tennis players led in the years between 1947, when Pancho Segura signed on to Jack Harris's professional tour, and 1968, the year tennis became open to all. For a start, interest in tennis was sporadic and unreliable and mostly still dominated by the wealthy elite lawn tennis clubs, which did not allow the "wrong sort," however good at tennis they may have been, into their memberships. There was no television to bring the game to a mass audience. There were no advertising endorsements to glamorize players and turn them into stars. There were no resorts or vacation complexes that might attract eager tennis students with the promise of meeting and taking lessons from champion players. There were no downtown programs to teach tennis to underprivileged kids and thus develop a following for the sport, as happened later, with great success, in basketball. Tennis programs at colleges and universities were small, few, and far between, and created little impact in the growing business of intervarsity sports.

It was in this climate of resistance and ignorance, and with little financial enticement for promoters or investors, that Pancho Segura and his teammates set off to change the world's perception of tennis.

The opening event of Jack Harris's newly formed tour took place at Madison Square Garden on December 26, 1947. There had been a snowstorm, and most transportation was cancelled, but in spite of the weather, over fifteen thousand fans turned out to see the now-legendary Bobby Riggs and his newly minted professional teammates play on a wooden surface laid over the ice-hockey rink—a typical adjustment for pro tennis at that time, regardless of how cold the players' feet might feel (particularly on a snowy winter night). Dinny Pails beat Pancho Segura in the opening match in an epic endurance test. The score of the first set was 15–13, but because of its immense length they had to stop the match to make time for the headliners. Then Bobby Riggs and Jack Kramer came onto the court, and Riggs beat the new star in a surprisingly tough 6–2, 10–8, 4–6, 6–4 struggle.

Immediately afterward the four men took a train to Pittsburgh and played the whole thing over again, Pails and Riggs again edging out their rivals. Thus the tour shaped up. It was always the same. Pails and Segura would play the warm-up match, then Riggs and Kramer played the headlined singles, and then the four men, usually Kramer and Segura versus Riggs and Pails, would play doubles. The players pushed on across the country as far as Florida and Arizona. On a wooden court in Tucson, the tide turned when Kramer beat Riggs in a marathon contest that lasted over four hours and ended at 1:30 in the morning with a final score of 14–12, 4–6, 18–16.

This was the form of the pro tour that Segura was to participate in for the next few years. Jack Kramer called Segura and Pails "the animal act." The two men were paid three hundred dollars a week for opening the "Duel of the Decade" tour, as it was called. In contrast, on that opening night in Madison Square Garden alone, Jack Kramer made $8,800 and Bobby Riggs made $4,400. It was very unfair," Kramer admitted. "But if you wanted to play professionally, it was the only game in town." (Bobby Riggs renegotiated his contract after beating Kramer that night in New York.)

The deal with Jack Harris was that he would pay all intercity transportation. Originally, the players traveled by train, but as the distances grew and train schedules were less convenient, they switched to cars. (Air travel was then in its infancy.) Jack Harris found a good deal on two DeSoto station wagons for them. He threw in fifty dollars a week for gas and incidentals for Kramer and Riggs. "That helped the kids in the animal act," Kramer conceded, "since they could ride with us."

They traveled constantly, extensively, night after night to a new place, with new conditions, through Europe, Asia, South America, even back to Pancho's home country, Ecuador. When promoter Jack Harris got sick, his four musketeers continued on without him, arranging their own tour of Australia and New Zealand, playing in countless towns in the two countries during the fall of 1948.

They were young, enthusiastic, and hungry. They were playing the game they loved. But the conditions were stressful, often exhausting. They traveled in the two station wagons, with a van behind carrying the equipment required to play tennis—two folding canvas panels for the court, a net, line markers, rackets, balls, and souvenir programs. (In those struggling years of professional tennis, no company would even sponsor their tennis-ball supply.) Jack Harris would travel with them for some of the way then go on ahead as advance man, hoping to drum up local interest in an attempt to get a gate that would pay off financially.

Jack Kramer, who right from the start was trying to work out how to make better money as a professional, described to tennis author and player Gene Scott the economics of the tour in those early days:

The normal split—almost everywhere but Madison Square Garden, which always demanded more from everybody—was 55/45. Our cut was 55 percent of the gross, while the arena got to keep 45 percent. The local promoter also had to pay all the expenses. We made a few more bucks sometimes selling souvenir programs. Right after the war, when I first started touring, the government had a special 20 percent amusement tax, and so there was a strict accounting of all tickets sold. But once the tax went off, you were very vulnerable to the local promoters taking advantage of you. It was tedious work, but the only way to make sure that you were getting a fair shake was to get a manifest of all the tickets printed and then count the dead wood—the tickets not sold—when the matches were through.

Sometimes a local promoter would take a bath and then you had to make a difficult decision. Should you let him pay you less than the guarantee? Jack Harris, my first promoter, taught me as a rule of thumb that if the guy had tried and if you thought you'd like to come back again and you could use this man, then let him off the book. Better to take some of the heat and give the guy a break if you could be sure he would work extra hard for you next time around.

As Kramer was the first to admit,

The finances of the whole tour were cuckoo. In the U.S. and Canada, you had to play four and a half matches a week to break even. Ideally, at a faster pace—five matches a week for ten weeks, fifty matches or so—it would be perfect for the promoter. But that was never enough once we were paying for other people we needed on the tour. Worse, once you had played ten weeks, you had almost certainly hit all the major markets. You might try to double back into a large city twice if you had a really top attraction, but generally speaking the act only played once. So after the first ten weeks, you were not only promoting just to break even, but you were doing it in high-school gyms in small towns.

Mostly they played indoors, because as the events were one-night stands, they could not take a chance on the weather. (Only in Florida or California could they play outdoors.) They were booked into a new place every night, every week. Each venue was different—a school auditorium, an opera house, a hockey rink, a town hall, a gymnasium. "We played the opera house in Saratoga, New York, once," Jack Kramer recalled, "where the back wall was eighteen inches from the baseline." The canvas surface indoors made for a fast game; the ball would sit up a little, like on grass. "The floor that went over the ice at the Montreal Forum was the one I remember the most because it was the worst of any big building," Kramer said. "It fit together all wrong. The sockets were worn. We'd aim for the holes."

The players were like a traveling band of actors, putting up a theater set for a one-night show, then striking it, loading it, and driving on to the next place, maybe hundreds of miles away, usually in the middle of the night. "We were too keyed up to sleep then, but if we waited till morning we had to get up early to get to the next town and get in all our publicity engagements," Kramer explained. On one occasion, after a long and exhausting overnighter on the road, the van driver transporting the tennis equipment got into an accident and was killed.

They would stay in cheap rooms—since there was no budget to speak of, who could argue? (Segura remembered occasionally having to sleep in the car.) They would scavenge for food, hoping to find some coffee shop open in the dead of night or early morning. They would sleep at odd hours, physically exhausted but pumped with adrenaline from the constant challenge of the competition. They would try to keep fit during the long trips on the road. There was never any time to rest. Maybe the next place would bring in a modest crowd—a few keen tennis fans who had actually heard of the great champions about to play for them. The bigger the gate, the better the pay.

But in some of the more out-of-the-way spots, there was no gate at all, and money had to be returned. Pancho remembered a time they traveled to Scotland. The event was to take place in Paisley, near Glasgow (a very rough, working-class district). Their promoter, Jack Harris, was full of optimism about this particular venue. "He said, 'Oh, I'm of Scottish ancestry, we're going to draw big,'" Segura related. "So we went there and there were only about a hundred people and we had to give the money back!"

And then there were the wives. Jack Kramer's wife, Gloria, had her hands full at home, raising four young boys, and did not usually travel with her husband. Dinny Pails's wife, Mavis, stayed home in Australia. Bobby Riggs was married to Kay, his supportive first wife who sometimes accompanied him on the road. When Frank Parker joined the tour at the end of 1949 he brought along his second wife, Audrey, who was older than he was. "Segura would always sneak up behind the Parkers as we came through customs so he could try to peek at Audrey's passport to find out exactly how much older than Frankie she was."

And Pancho brought Virginia.

"I never knew Pancho had got married," Jack Kramer said," until he showed up with this pretty girl at his side." Kramer laughed at the memory. "He was very jealous," he continued. "Often Virginia was the only woman traveling in the car with us, and Pancho would make quite sure she sat by the window with him next to her, so there was no chance for anyone else to try any funny stuff."

Pancho's difficulties were aggravated by the fact that at the beginning he could not drive, so the others had to do most of the driving. "We decided to teach Pancho to drive," Kramer said, "and at the motels we stayed at, every morning we would take him to one of our cars and make him sit in the driver's seat and learn to drive right there in the parking lot. It got quite dangerous after we let him on the road, he'd almost be leaning out of the window to make sure he was seeing right. He was scared to death in the early days—and so were we!"

Virginia loved those first years of the tour, not surprisingly, since she was young and adventurous and traveling to exciting places with her new husband and several other attractive and athletic young men. "I'd go to all their matches," she said, "I loved the action, just being out there."

Of course it wasn't like the amateur tour. No ambassadors came to meet them or invite them to their grand houses or dine with them in expensive restaurants. Usually only a scrappy local gatekeeper showed up to take them to the place where they were to play and then left them alone. Virginia wasn't so sure about the hotel rooms either. "They smelled like cigarette smoke," she recalled. "And you got athlete's foot if you walked around on the carpet without your shoes." She laughed. "But we weren't in them much. Sometimes we didn't get to bed till three o'clock in the morning and then we had to be up again at eight."

She admitted that the pace was grueling. "One night I was in the bathtub and trying to take a bath and Pancho came in, saying, 'You're not ready to go to the game?' And I said, 'Yes, oh, yes, wait, wait, of course I want to go.' But instead I lay back and burst into tears."

After that, Virginia went home for a rest.

Even if at times Virginia found the tour overwhelming, she still loved it—because Pancho loved it. Pancho was transformed as a person and as a player by his years on the tour. "I was happy because I was doing something I loved," he said simply.

For Pancho, the travel was stimulating, thrilling. It widened his horizons. "I was always interested in each town we went to, finding out about the people, how they lived, how they earned their money. In England, for instance, I studied all the places we went to. What made them work? Manchester, an industrial city. Blackpool, the political party base. My biggest thrill was meeting Clement Attlee, the first postwar prime minister after Winston Churchill, who came to Wembley to see us play in 1949."

Pancho knew who Attlee was. He had started taking an interest in politics when he was still a student at Miami and read newspapers and newsweeklies voraciously. "I was in Coral Gables practicing my tennis when Roosevelt made the speech about Pearl Harbor in 1941," he recalled. "I was very big on current events even then. It was one of my biggest assets." So when he was in England, he knew all sorts of things about British politics and why it was interesting to play tennis for Clement Attlee. He knew about Benjamin Disraeli, Anthony Eden, especially Neville Chamberlain, "the appeaser," who tried to avoid World War II. Pancho read all the time, in the car, in the bus, in the train, learning about the places where he was going to play tennis. And when he had found out all he could, he went on to the court and played.

He raised his tennis to another level during those first years of the tour. "The guy who won got more money than the one who lost, so that was an incentive," he said later. "We played to win." Each time they arrived in a new place, they practiced, because the conditions were always terrible. If they were in some school gymnasium or town hall, Pancho would sneak out by himself and start lobbing the ball up into the rafters to see how easy it would be to see when the lights were on. "The glare of the lights made it difficult."

Jack Kramer saw this intensity in the little Ecuadorian. "No matter whom Pancho was playing, winning and losing was like death and taxes to him. He just couldn't stand the idea of losing, and so he put out the maximum to keep from losing, and that's why his consistency was so damn good."

The financial lure was certainly a major factor in the desire to win, but for Pancho there was another incentive. He wanted to improve his game. That was always in his mind, to improve his game. He wanted to be a better tennis player. "You improved because you had to. I used to run. I used machines. I played against the wall to practice volleys. Practice first from a standing position, then on the run. In a game, nobody is going to hit the ball back to you. So you must master balls coming from corner to corner."

Pancho's speed was legendary. Just as Jack Kramer had learned from playing him before the war, Pancho could wear down anybody who did not protect himself. But he still had to prove he had staying power. Playing on the tour, Pancho figured out that he had to pace himself, to be willing to allow crosscourt or down-the-line shots that were coming to his weaker stroke. "My backhand was my weakness, compared to my forehand, and the other guys knew it, so it improved because they played it all the time. It had to improve. And I lasted longer."

Pancho was always focused on improving his game, and the tour experience was ideal for his purpose. To play great players night after night was the perfect way to learn to play better. Jack Kramer taught him to keep some of his energy in reserve and to build on his serve. Kramer's huge serve and volley—the "big game" as it was called—had transformed tennis; rushing to the net behind a big serve and putting away the return with a volley was by this time part of the repertoire of every competitive player. "We played indoors," Pancho said, "which is very fast, so the guy with the big serve has a big advantage. With no fresh air, the ball doesn't get heavy. I had to compensate for that."

Kramer's dueling rival, Bobby Riggs, was equally useful to Pancho. Bobby was short, like Pancho, and bantam light compared to Kramer and Budge. But he used to win his matches with a combination of anticipation, speed, and an armory of cunning strategy. "I learned a lot from Bobby," Pancho said. "Not about hustling—though there was never better—but about playing to win. Bobby had every shot in the book and nerves of steel. He could beat you from the back because he was so quick and had a beautiful game. He was a baseline player, but playing Kramer he decided he had to come to the net. He used his head. He was a little guy playing a big guy—just like I was."

Thanks to Bobby's inspirational court technique, Pancho got much better at tennis. "Bobby and I only weighed 140 pounds, against Kramer and the other guys weighing 175 or more," he explained, "and they had the advantage of height when they served. But we had the advantage when we were on the move, running around the court. We were the roadrunners of the tennis world."

At some point, Pancho changed his grip. Aware that his backhand was his weakest stroke, he studied Kramer's and copied the master's continental grip. "I oversliced the ball, I would cut it, so that it would go high, and the other guy would rush to the net and volley it away from me. By changing to a continental grip I kept the ball lower so he could not put it away so easily. I had to do this since we all played a net game and my old backhand was no good for that kind of play." Changing your grip takes hard work and concentration, but for Pancho there was never any question that he must do it. "If you hold your racket badly, you can play the rest of your life and never improve." His dedication paid off, and his backhand became much stronger. Not that it was ever as good as his forehand. Jack Kramer often said that he thought Segura's two-handed forehand was the best shot in the game. During these years of hard, intensive play and constant self-improvement, Pancho became fit, hard, and firm, "like iron." In 1949 he began playing Kramer on even terms.

But perhaps even more than the tennis, people began to come to see "Segoo," as friends in the game called him, for his extraordinary personality on the court. The eager, lopsided walk, the wiry frame, the laserlike strokes, the sense of humor, the twinkling eyes and flashing smile, combined to make Segura the darling of the fans. He would urge himself on during long points, calling out, *"Ahora, Pancho, ahora! Vamos!"* ("Now, Pancho, now! Let's go!"), as he charged the net or pulled off a sneaky concealed drop shot. (That was another name the players gave him—"Sneaky.") Today, of course, shouts and grunts are commonplace, but in those days Pancho's utterances were quite startling to audiences, for whom tennis was still a gentleman's game, with no show of emotion and no noises allowed. "Tennis was so quiet always," Pancho said, laughing.

It was not only talking to himself that endeared him to the fans. After a particularly brilliant shot, he would turn to the applauding crowds and tap the side of his head, grinning hugely, inviting their adoration, just as a decade later, his protégé Jimmy Connors, after making a winner, would look up at the stands and defiantly pump his fist in triumph. "I'd tell my opponent I'm a showman," Pancho said, "They usually knew that. I was like a contortionist. In South Africa I'd clown and clap in front of the Indian group in the stands. They loved it. They loved me being the little guy against the big gringo." Pancho had become a performer, and the audiences were delighted by him.

The big gringo, Jack Kramer, was quick to appreciate the magical and moneymaking power of his teammate: "The fans would come out to see the new challenger face the old champion," he said, "but they would leave talking about the bandy-legged little sonovabitch who gave them such pleasure playing the first match and the doubles. The next time the tour came to town the fans would come back to see Segoo."

In 1949 Bobby Riggs took over the promotion of the tour from Jack Harris. While Harris had been an important public relations and front man, both Kramer and Riggs, Harris's major money-makers, felt that their contracts were inadequate. Riggs, always the gambler of the group, suggested to Kramer that they cut Harris out entirely and manage the tour on their own, with Riggs's wife, Kay, doing the public relations and advance work. Kramer agreed. Segura and Pails also signed on, for marginally better money.

The newly formed group set off on an arduous schedule of appearances, beginning with a European tour of England, Scotland, Spain, France, Belgium, Italy, and Denmark. At Wembley, in March, Segura beat Pails decisively, winning three matches to none, the second two matches going to only two sets, 6–4, 6–4, and 6–2, 6–3. Two months later, at the London Indoor Pro Champs, Jack Kramer beat Bobby Riggs in front of twenty-four thousand fans by the score of 2–6, 6–4, 6–3, 6–4. But more significantly, Segura held Kramer off in a semifinal duel that went to five sets, 3–6, 6–3, 6–3, 3–6, 6–3. (By this time nobody could accuse Pancho of not having staying power!)

In December, 1949, the Inca Warrior showed his increasingly threatening competitiveness on the court by defeating the newest pro on the tour, Frank Parker, twice, in the World Championship series at Wembley. Parker had just won the French singles and doubles and the Wimbledon doubles championships, as well as being a regular Davis Cup player since 1937. Segura was not fazed by this impressive record. His scores were a convincing 7–5, 6–2, and 6–2, 6–3. (By the end of the 1950 tour, Pancho had beaten Parker fifty-seven straight times.) A month after crushing Parker in London, Pancho reached a tennis pinnacle of sorts in the Paris Pro Indoors, when he pulled off a stunning victory over Jack Kramer in two sets, 6–3, 6–2. This triumph, recorded in January 1950, heralded the beginning of Segura's greatest years on the professional tour.

It also coincided with the appearance of another player who was later to dominate the game throughout the world. He was tall, dark, Hollywood-handsome, and a dazzling performer on the tennis court, a Mexican-American whose moods became as famous as his huge serve. His name was Richard Gonzales, and he was to play a dramatic role in Segura's life for the next ten years.

Chapter Six A New Contender

By the middle of 1949, Bobby Riggs was burned out. Having been beaten by Kramer an embarrassing number of times—69-20 matches at the end of the 1948 North American tour—Riggs had pulled himself together enough to win the U.S. Professional Championships at Forest Hills against Don Budge. But his best playing days were over, and his fans were losing interest. Jack Kramer's star was in the ascendancy, and the tour had only served to enhance the younger man's image, while Riggs admitted that he was depressed and exhausted.

So Bobby Riggs, never one to flinch before a big gamble, retired his tennis racket at the age of thirty-one. But he wasn't finished with tennis by any means. With Jack Harris out of the picture, he saw a chance to stay in the game as a promoter. Working with Jack Kramer as his prime draw and business partner, maybe they'd make some money. But without Riggs on the marquee, they needed new blood from the amateur ranks to replace him, and there seemed only two possibilities—Ted Schroeder and Richard Gonzales.

Schroeder, Jack Kramer's friend and doubles partner, had been ranked among the top ten in the United States and world for many years, as well as having won the doubles title several times at Forest Hills. He was known for his courage and stamina and was a stalwart presence during many years of Davis Cup play. Gonzales was another matter altogether. Only twenty-one in 1949, he had exploded on the scene in a major way by winning the U.S. championship and clay-court titles in 1948. Yet in a series of practice matches against Don Budge in Los Angeles, he only won one set out of twenty-five matches. He also had a poor record against

Schroeder. Moreover, his background and reputation made him a risky bet under any circumstances.

A few weeks before Wimbledon in the summer of 1949, Riggs and Kramer met Schroeder at the Athenaeum Court Hotel in London to make a deal. Schroeder agreed to turn pro for a fee of twenty-five thousand dollars, regardless of the gate. (Kramer had earned eighty-nine thousand dollars from the previous year's tour.) Two weeks later Schroeder called off the deal. Riggs and Kramer were furious, but they could not dissuade him. They were faced with the only possible alternative—about whom they were still very doubtful—Richard Gonzales.

Gonzales had just lost in a badly played fourth-round match at Wimbledon, after which tennis writer Jim Burchard called him the cheese champ. The name was picked up by the players, who called him the gorgonzola cheese champ, then and forever shortened to "Gorgo." "It's a little ridiculous that one of the best players in history has a nickname derived from his being a bum," Jack Kramer commented, "but it was one of the few things that never bothered Gonzales."

So who was this gorgonzola cheese champ? What were Riggs and Kramer to do, signing a rather unreliable Gorgo to their first tour together?

Richard Gonzales was born in Los Angeles on May 9, 1928. His parents were both Mexican. His father, Manuel Antonio Gonzalez, and grandfather, José, came to the United States from Durango when Manuel was nine years old, fleeing the infamous 1918 influenza epidemic that killed Manuel's mother, his twin sisters, and three other siblings. After an arduous trek across the desert (mostly barefoot), they finally arrived in Globe, Arizona, a small mining town near Phoenix, where Richard's great-uncle was struggling to survive in crushing poverty.

Richard's mother, Carmen Esperanza Alire, also migrated from Mexico. Her background was far superior to her husband's. She would talk about the land her family owned in the city and outskirts of Chihuahua, and the loving childhood she had enjoyed, surrounded by wealth and comfort. But the wealth did not last, and she moved to Los Angeles in about 1927, when she was seventeen years old, along with her parents and four sisters, to escape the political instability back home and to find a better life in California. It was in Los Angeles, shortly after the Alires arrived, that Carmen Esperanza met Manuel Antonio. The young couple fell in love and married.

The Alire family was surely not thrilled by the choice. Manuel Gonzales was short and wiry, and he always seemed to get into trouble, often because of drink. (He changed the last letter of his name from z to s to help gringos pronounce it properly.) He worked at various jobs and was not always reliable with the paycheck. He was very house-proud, however, helping fix up their modest place when Carmen became pregnant with her first child, Richard. Carmen was a handsome woman, with an imperious bearing, as though conscious of her upscale past. "She had this striking Indian beauty," her son Ralph said, "that made most people move out of her way when she was coming down the street."

Richard's birth was followed by twins Manuel Jr. and Margaret in 1929, Ophelia (later Teri) in 1930, Bertha in 1931, Ralph in 1933, and Yolanda, a late baby, in 1942. They all lived in East Los Angeles, now better known as South Central L.A. Added to this large number was José, Manuel's father, who came to live with them when Richard was a small boy. The times were hard. It was the middle of the Depression, and Richard's father was hardly able to provide for his large family, let alone his father. At one point, the situation was so bad that Manuel took all the family back to Mexico, to his wife's town, Chihuahua. But things were worse there, and they returned—leaving a daughter, Margaret, behind.

With his father constantly out trying to find work, José, Richard's grandfather, played an important role in Richard's young life. He was a trained carpenter and taught his grandson Richard to make kites, tops, and model airplanes. He also taught him how to play marbles, at which the little boy became an expert, soon beating all the other boys on the street. His competitive spirit, it seems, was apparent at an early age

In 1935, at the age of seven, Richard suffered an accident that would mark him for life. Racing out into the street on a scooter to play marbles with a friend, he crashed head first into the side of a car. The car was designed with large protruding door handles, and the boy's cheek was crushed by the handle, "blowing the left side of his face out," as his brother Ralph later described it. Richard survived, but the scar on his cheek was permanent.

Mrs. Gonzales was shattered by her eldest son's disfigurement. There was a Mexican song she knew about Juan Charrasquiado, Scarface John, a bad character, and she kept thinking of gangster Al Capone, who also had a scar. She felt that Richard would be scarred, not only by the wound but by the impression of criminality conveyed to gringos by the mark on his cheek. "Mom began a daily ritual of spreading Mexican cocoa butter on Richard's scar for years," Ralph wrote in his memoir, "in the hopes of blending the scar into a nice chocolate brown so it wouldn't be so noticeable." Richard hated it—"it made me smell like chocolate."

Oddly, Richard himself seems not to have been distressed by the scar. As Jack Kramer said about Richard's later nickname, "Gorgo," some things simply did not bother him. Richard's vanity, such as it was, was not about his appearance. Of course when Richard became a famous tennis champion, the scar on his cheek was an important aspect of his image as a romantic, dangerous personality.

As Richard grew up, his unruly and undisciplined nature emerged in ways that enraged his father, with whom he had countless rows, and from whom he received beatings and punishments as well. Manuel Gonzales was a strict disciplinarian, with a hot temper, and he was permanently worried abut money, so his eldest son's irresponsibility and rebelliousness both at school and at home drove him crazy. But Richard was a good student, so good in fact that he skipped fifth grade, and although he seemed never to do homework, he brought home A's.

Richard was not athletic as a child. He was not a fast runner, and he later told his brother that when he was young he was afraid he was never going to be fast enough to be a good athlete. Where he could compete with anybody was in playing marbles, and he played for money and won. A defining story of Richard's ambition, told by Ralph, concerns the day Richard saw a black man putting on a marbles exhibition in the park—but he had no arms. He shot the marbles with his feet, and beat most of the people who challenged him. "I don't know how many times I heard [my brother] say that this changed his life," Ralph said. "If this man with this enormous handicap could accomplish what he had and keep smiling, then he, Richard, could do anything he set his mind to."

The other defining story concerns Richard's discovery of tennis. His mother explained that one day they were at the movies and there was a news clip about a tennis champion (probably Bill Tilden). Richard was transfixed by watching him play tennis, saying, "Some day I'm going to be a champion like that!" His mother also took him to the park where he saw people play tennis. Perhaps it's not surprising that his mother encouraged this interest—to her, with her consciousness of class and background, tennis was a gentleman's game and therefore suitable for her son to take up. "When I was a little girl in Mexico," she told a reporter, "the people next door were very wealthy and their children played tennis. Because I didn't have any of those things, I wanted Richard to have them. Also I didn't want him playing any rough games like football where he might get hurt."

In 1940 Richard's mother gave him a fifty-cent tennis racket for Christmas. It was the turning point. He picked it up and, in a sense, never put it down again. He started playing wherever he could, hitting balls against garage walls, on the street, wearing out the strings almost immediately. (He quickly repaired them with silk gut bought from Sears.) He sometimes even slept with his racket. He found a partner in Chuck Pate, a regular tennis player who played with the younger boy and began explaining to him the rudimentary points of the game. Soon Richard became good enough for Chuck to start using him as a ringer in tournaments.

But the biggest break came when Frank Poulain, owner of a tennis shop and hamburger stand in Exposition Park, saw Richard play. Poulain at once spotted the Mexican boy's talent and invited him to play at the park. "Expo," as it was called, became the center of Richard's life for the next few years. Poulain encouraged him to work at the game, taught him strategy, and put him up against the best players who would hang out at Expo, betting a burger that he would win. Richard ate a lot of burgers!

Ralph later perceptively described the relationship between Poulain and Gonzales. "There was a magnetic attraction for both of them. Frank saw the greatness in this young dark-skinned kid, and he treated him with an understanding that Richard had not known at home. Being a hustler, Frank understood Richard's thirst for competitive challenges. . . . It was a father-son type of relationship." The two men would hang out with friends and play poker and gin rummy, as well as tennis, and every day Richard refined his skills, both athletic and mental. He found he could make money in the process. He was becoming a canny gambler and a very good tennis player.

Needless to say, his father hated the fact that his eldest son spent all his time at Expo either playing a sissy game or gambling and frittering his time away with bums. On one occasion, in a rage he broke one of Richard's rackets over his knee. "Go ahead! Break the other if you like!" Richard screamed. "Tomorrow I'll be back with two more!"

Richard would duck out of school and disappear for days. He would get arrested for being out after curfew. His father would beat him unmercifully for these infractions, often with a razor strap, a big belt, or an electric cord. The worst punishment seemed more like torture: Manuel would tie strings to each of his son's thumbs and hang him from the garage ceiling. "My arms and shoulders cramped; my legs ached from standing so long; my thumbs were numb." But Richard didn't care. He ran right back downtown to Expo and his buddies.

Meanwhile, the work on the tennis courts paid off. When Richard was nearly fifteen, he was already six foot two and a formidable opponent on the court. He began winning local and state tournaments. He often found himself competing against a player who was also gaining a lot of attention, Herbert (Herbie) Flam. Richard won every final in which they were pitted against each other. Tennis writers began to take an interest. In 1943, Richard was ranked the number one player in his fifteen-and-under age group for Southern California by the Southern California Tennis Association (SCTA).

This meant not only honor, but automatic representation at the Junior Nationals. But instead of nominating him, the SCTA nominated Herbie Flam, ranked number two. Their excuse was that Richard's poor school attendance made him ineligible. The ruling was imposed by the secretary of the SCTA, Perry T. Jones, and in spite of an outcry (including the claim of racism) from Frank Poulain and others, the ruling stood. "Richard spent that night on his knees crying with his head on Mom's lap," Ralph recalled.

Richard's response was anger and defiance. He continued to play hooky from school and began doing petty crime, in particular, burglary. Perry Jones continued to punish his star, ultimately banning him from all SCTA-sanctioned tournaments, wherever and whenever they were played. At last things reached a crisis point. The police arrested Richard for curfew violations, and he then confessed to several burglaries. In front of his father, who was unable to defend his boy, Richard was sentenced to jail. It was 1944, two months before his sixteenth birthday. For his father, it was a humiliating admission that he could not control his son. For his mother, it was a devastating blow to have to admit her son was a jailbird. Richard spent nine months in Preston Reform School and was released in December 1945.

With bleak prospects, a failed education, and barred from competitive tennis, Richard joined the Marines. He had no better success there, for he hated the rules and restrictions, he couldn't play tennis, and when he came home on leave he decided not to go back. He was court-martialed for being absent without leave, sent to the brig, and finally released in January 1947, after eighteen months.

At this low point, only one ambition lingered in Richard's

mind—to play tennis. He started training again—seriously, this time. That is, he spent his days playing tennis at Expo. "His training also included late nights, hustling gin rummy, shooting snooker, and bowling," Ralph commented. In short, Richard Gonzales had no idea how to train. He trained by playing tennis, day after day, against anyone who had the gall to challenge him, and beat his body by night, gambling and driving fast cars. Poulain again entered him in the scta tournament in May, and again Jones and his cronies refused his application, but this time, as Richard was nineteen and considered an adult, they had no grounds to deny him and they reluctantly allowed him into the tournament.

The tournament was played at the Los Angeles Tennis Club, which, at that time, was one of the most exclusive clubs in California. It rivaled the Beverly Hills Tennis Club for glamour, with Hollywood stars such as Humphrey Bogart, Ava Gardner, Errol Flynn, and many other movie greats of the time showing up there to play tennis. It was also where Jack Kramer first honed his talent as a junior in the late 1930s.

While Gonzales had been out of action, his longtime rival Herbie Flam had been winning most of the trophies on the California amateur tennis circuit. As fate would have it, Richard drew Flam in the first round of the tournament. Perry Jones was delighted. He thought that Gonzales, with no practice, no training, and no experience, would take a terrible beating from Flam and the humiliation would finish the Mexican upstart's career for good.

Gonzales won the match in three sets, 8–10, 8–6, 6–4. Nobody could believe it. People had not seen Gonzales for several years, and many fans hardly knew who he was. The Los Angeles Times called the victory a classic, as Gonzales "stepped out of tennis oblivion in dramatic fashion" to participate in the championship. "Six times in the second set Flam held match points, but Gonzales served booming aces five of the times and on the sixth he passed his foe with a backhand crosscourt."

His quarterfinal match was against Jack Kramer, already a seasoned champion. This time Gonzales showed his inexperience.

Kramer's power and needle-sharp accuracy caught his opponent off guard, and he beat Gonzales in four sets, 6–2, 6–4, 3–6, 6–3. But the defeat was not really a defeat for the young player. Reporters noted how he was a gallery favorite, with his "steaming serves and dashes to the net." His friends from Expo cheered him wildly from the stands, and everyone else who had never heard of him started talking about the new talent on the court. He had comported himself brilliantly throughout the tournament, and now Perry Jones himself was prepared to concede that, although a Latino, Gonzales would be an important addition to the teams sponsored by the SCTA.

That summer Richard played in several tournaments, each time improving his play, until he reached the American pinnacle of amateur competition, the U.S. Lawn Tennis Championship at Forest Hills. He lost in the second round, in a close five-set battle against one of the great tennis players of all time, Gardnar Mulloy. When he went home after that match, Ralph remembered his brother saying, "These guys are not really that good." Gonzales was beginning to measure himself against the great ones and sense that one day, not so far in the future, he would beat them.

He gave the world notice very shortly after Forest Hills. In September 1947, he entered the major West Coast tournament, the Pacific Southwest Tennis Championships, in Los Angeles. It attracted all the best players, including Jack Kramer, who had just won the Wimbledon and U.S. Open singles titles, Frank Parker, Ted Schroeder, Bob Falkenberg, the 1946 Wimbledon champion, Jaroslav Drobny, the European champion, and a little Ecuadorian called Pancho Segura.

Richard Gonzales faced off against these established stars and in the space of three days defeated Drobny, Falkenberg, and Parker. A reporter said, "The ovation Gonzales received from spectators after defeating Parker could be heard clear to the Pacific Ocean." Fans began comparing him to Bill Tilden and Don Budge. Who was this nineteen-year-old, dark-skinned, lanky kid, who appeared out of the blue to decimate these great players? His photograph was on the front page of the *Los Angeles Herald*. His mother basked in her son's glory.

Richard reached the semifinal, where his opponent was Ted Schroeder. After a tough battle, Schroeder won in four sets. But like the U.S. Open, the defeat was nothing compared to the new-found fame Gonzales had gained for himself. The fans loved him, the women adored him, and the men recognized a rival who could outmatch them on and off the court. Richard's haunting face, wide smile, pantherlike movements, and athletic performance brought new excitement and sexiness to a game that badly needed it.

In 1948 Gonzales joined the Eastern circuit as the seventeenth ranked player in the United States. To everyone's surprise, he also got married. His bride was Henrietta Pedrin, who was pregnant with their first child. His parents, particularly his mother, were horrified, but Richard did not care. He had found a new life with a new family and for the first time felt free from his domineering father.

His tennis continued to improve. In March 1948 he won the National Clay Court title by beating Bill Talbert 10–8, 6–0, 4–6, 9–7. This was a new achievement for him, playing against another great top ten U.S. player, and on an unfamiliar surface. The tennis year would again climax with the Forest Hills championship, and this time Gonzales was seeded number eight.

The seeding committee must have regretted that one. Gonzales blazed through the tournament like a fireball, beating the number one seed, Frank Parker, the Czech champion, Drobny, and finally winning the title against the South African, Eric Sturgess, in three straight sets, 6–2, 6–3, 14–12. Once again the tennis world was stunned.

In the Pacific Southwest tournament, after this great triumph, Schroeder, Richard's nemesis, beat him again. (Not for the first time, the accusation was raised that Gonzales only won the U.S. title because Schroeder wasn't playing.) In December of that year, Richard's first-born son, Richard Jr., was born. By this time, the young champion was losing ground. He continued to hang out at Expo, and put on weight, gaining 125 pounds. "Amateur tennis's No. 1 Bad Boy is also its No. 1 Star," wrote tennis writer Gene Farmer. They again began calling him the cheese champ.

In the summer of 1949 Gonzales went to Europe to play in the French Championship and other European tournaments. They were not a success. The kid from West Central L.A. had never been to Europe, let alone flown on an international flight or stayed in a first-class hotel. He was put up at one of the grander Parisian hotels, the George V, where he had no idea how to handle room service, let alone the press who bombarded his hotel room at all hours of the day and night.

But in spite of being less than 100 percent fit, jet-lagged, and unfamiliar with the heavy European tennis balls, which were not pressurized, he got as far as the singles semifinals of the French, losing to Budge Patty, and won the doubles with Frank Parker. Richard went on to Holland, Germany, and England, where Wimbledon once again presented a huge challenge. Richard, disappointingly, lost in the round of sixteen, and Ted Schroeder won, but again Richard hung in to win the doubles with his partner, Frank Parker, against Schroeder and Mulloy. Back in the States, Richard began to lose weight and win titles: he won the U.S. Clay Courts, the tournaments in Newport, Rhode Island, and in Southampton, at the Meadow Club, avenging his loss in the French Championship by beating Budge Patty.

It was at this point in his career that he was invited to play for the United States in the Davis Cup. Schroeder was the obvious first choice, but the second choice, to people's surprise, was Richard Gonzales. It was a long shot; admittedly Gonzales had won the U.S. Open in a surprise victory (and yes, Schroeder wasn't playing), but since then his record was unreliable. His weight and inconsistency were worrying. But in spite of all the doubts, Gonzales played well and helped the United States win the trophy. It was the one and only time he played Davis Cup, and it was one of the proudest moments of his life.

A few weeks later Schroeder and Gonzales met again in the finals of the U.S. Open at Forest Hills. Again, most people thought Schroeder, given his fine track record, would win easily. In spite of his Davis Cup showing, and in spite of holding the U.S. singles title, Gonzales still had not convinced the tennis community that he was a champion, and although seeded second, he was regarded by most observers as too unpredictable to win a major championship against such an experienced opponent. How wrong they were.

When it came to the final, the stadium at Forest Hills was packed. Schroeder was immensely popular, and his arrogant behavior on court was a provocation to the fans. The dark, athletic, and moody Gonzales made a thrilling and mysterious opponent. The first set stunned everyone. It was the longest set ever played in a final at Forest Hills. At one point Gonzales had triple set point on Schroeder's serve, before losing it, 18–16, in an agonizing hour and fifteen minutes. On a roll from that critical but draining victory, Schroeder raced to a two-set lead, 6–2.

According to Jack Kramer, the conventional wisdom would have been at this point for Schroeder to relax, let Gonzales work for the third set, then come back strongly and win the fourth and the match. Nobody held out the faintest hope for Gonzales, particularly since Schroeder had the maturity and stamina that Gonzales evidently lacked. But Gonzales stormed into the third set, tossing off the first four games, with Schroeder fighting furiously to get back into the set before losing it, 6–1. The fourth set was equally shocking. With Schroeder now getting increasingly rattled, Gonzales won comfortably, 6–2.

At two sets all, the match was clearly becoming a marathon and the fans were beside themselves with excitement. Was the giant killer going to get killed? How could Schroeder possibly lose after such a dazzling start? Gonzales never heard those questions. At four games all, after almost five hours of play, he reached deep down into himself and pulled out the set at 6–4. To win the match after being down by two bitterly fought sets was a staggering triumph for the twenty-one-year-old Gonzales.

"How Schroeder lost the match after the first set is beyond my comprehension," Jack Kramer wrote later. Kramer went on to suggest that Schroeder, maybe subconsciously, "tanked" the game as the convenient way out after his reneging on the deal to turn professional. Kramer remembered going into the locker room with Bobby Riggs after the game to commiserate, "And the first thing he said was, 'Now I guess everyone will be happy.'" Of course the Gonzales camp would have been outraged at such a despicable suggestion. Gonzales won a brilliant victory that day, and it was a turning point in his career. *Tennis Magazine* later picked this Gonzales-Schroeder final as one of the twenty greatest matches of all time.

Bobby Riggs wasted no time in finding out which plane Gonzales was flying back home to Los Angeles, and he wrangled his way on to the seat next to him. For most of the six-hour flight, Riggs worked his charm and powers of persuasion to induce Gonzales to turn pro. It must have been quite a scene, the small, button-faced tennis champion–promoter with the high-pitched voice talking up a deal to the tall, swarthy outrider from West Central L.A., as the plane flew over the Rockies. The two men had common ground however, apart from tennis: both were inveterate gamblers, and probably Bobby picked up on this weakness in his prey. But while Riggs would take a bet on anything that moved, the younger man was used to the world of two-bit, pool-hall contests. Never in his life had Richard Gonzales been offered the gamble that Riggs presented to him now—a contract to play tennis against the number one in the world, Jack Kramer. Of course he could not turn it down.

The new tour opened on October 25, 1949, at Madison Square Garden, to a huge and enthusiastic crowd. The deal was that Kramer and Gonzales would get 30 percent of the gate on top of their fee. Once again, Pails and Segura, without such attractive financial enticements, were lined up as the animal act. The result prefigured the disaster to follow. Kramer beat Gonzales easily, 6–4, 3–6, 6–3, 6–2. Of their twenty-six ensuing matches held throughout North America, Kramer won twenty-two, including Gonzales's most humiliating defeat in Waterloo, Ontario, of 6–1, 6–1.

It could hardly have been a more horrible start for Gonzales.

He was young and untested. He didn't understand the grinding schedule he would have to endure. He hated to lose those endless matches, night after night. His competitive spirit was bruised. The consistent losses eroded his confidence and turned his enjoyment in the game into anger and disappointment. Kramer asserted that he and Gonzales made seventy-three thousand dollars on the U.S.-Canada circuit (30 percent of the take), but added that for Gonzales, it was hardly worth the price he had to pay.

Besides learning the hard way about dealing with defeat over and over again on the court, Gonzales also sensed very quickly how much of an outsider he was, with Riggs and Kramer always with their heads together, plotting moneymaking schemes, leaving Gonzales on the sidelines. His background separated him from them, and he resented it. The problem was to become more and more intractable as time went on. The temperament and character of the new addition to the Riggs and Kramer dog-and-pony show had begun to take shape, and the results were not pretty. Richard Gonzales was growing up fast and beginning to see the pitfalls of playing a game that still carried a gentleman's exclusivity about it.

There was perhaps only one friend who might help him—another Latino, another émigré, a man who in many ways could hardly be more different, but who played tennis side-by-side with him every night on the road. If he was to survive this decision to turn pro, he was going to need Pancho Segura's help. Ironically, it was at this moment, while Gonzales's rising star suddenly seemed poised for a nosedive, that Segura's own career began to reach its pinnacle.

W ith the collapse of Gonzales, Bobby Riggs's tour was in deep trouble. No other amateur player was ready to turn pro and take on Jack Kramer. With Bobby out of the game, the cupboard was bare. Kramer wondered if they should start publicizing Pancho Segura, their most popular player, who had become very competitive in the most recent year of the tour. On New Year's Day of 1950, Segura beat Kramer handily in Paris with the score of 6–3, 6–2. He beat Kramer again in June in the semifinals of the U.S. Pro in a lengthy duel that showed its drama in the score: 6–4, 8–10, 1–6, 6–4, 6–3. (Segura went on to win the tournament against Kovacs.)

But as Kramer put it, "There was no way he could handle my serve. Hell, once I beat him nineteen in a row. Also, as entertaining as Segura could be, that wouldn't do us any good coming into a town, because he didn't come in with any amateur publicity—no Forest Hills or Wimbledon titles, no Davis Cup play." (This problem was to haunt Pancho all his life—turning pro before he could win those crown jewels.)

So Riggs and Kramer came up with a desperate solution. Bring in a woman. (The idea foreshadowed Bobby Riggs's later claim to marketing immortality by challenging a woman to play him in the "Match of the Century.") The obvious woman on the tennis circuit was Gertrude (Gussie) Moran. Lots of people had heard of Gussie Moran. She came from California and was ranked number four in the country after winning the National Indoor singles and doubles titles in 1949. But more to the point in marketing terms, she was long-legged, pretty, and—thanks to a provocative appearance at Wimbledon wearing lacy panties, unheard-of at the stodgy

All England Club—she had been dubbed "Gorgeous Gussie" by the British tabloids. Riggs and Kramer decided to pit her against Pauline Betz, not as well known, but a far better tennis player. Betz was 1946 Wimbledon singles champion and four-time national champion at Forest Hills.

The two ladies would appear first, and then Kramer would go up against Segura as the all-guy event. For the first time, Segura had a stake in the tour—one thousand dollars a week plus 5 percent of the gate. Kramer took a smaller cut than usual—only 25 percent of the gate—in order to get Gussie Moran. Bobby as promoter had the best deal—40 percent. Pauline Betz was paid a straight fee.

The opening match at Madison Square Garden on October 28, 1950, was yet another disaster. Gorgeous Gussie, expected to deliver the sexpot image the audiences had been promised, appeared in very low-key, conventional tennis clothes, while Pauline startled the fans by showing up in silver lamé shorts and a bright pink sweater. Having annihilated Gussie in the fashion department, Pauline went on to annihilate her on the tennis court, 6–0, 6–3, in just over half an hour. The male performers did little better in competitive terms—Kramer easily beat Segura.

At this all-important opener, there was no excitement, no tension, nothing. Moreover, in spite of all the publicity Riggs attracted, the gate was surprisingly small—only 6,526 people showed up to see this oddball entertainment. As Kramer said later, "Tennis fans come to see tennis." Lacking competitive championship play to present to audiences, Riggs's publicity stunts did not pay off. (Later it was said that this bad experience prejudiced people against women's tennis. Ironically Riggs himself helped change all that with his famous defeat at the hands of Billie Jean King just over twenty years later in 1973.)

The badly matched foursome traveled on to other cities, but the scores were the same, even after Kramer begged Pauline to try and make her matches with Gussie a little more competitive. After a while it was decided that the women should only play one set, but it made no difference. The fans stayed away in droves. With no advance ticket money, the tour ended up just about bankrupt. It closed in March 1951, having grossed just over ninety-four thousand dollars, not even a third of the figure collected during the Riggs-Kramer "Duel of the Decade" tour.

As for Pancho, the Gussie Moran experiment was merely a distraction. All he cared about was tennis. "We were pioneers of the game," he said. "I wanted to play tennis, that's all. I would think about it all the time, eat, sleep, dream tennis." Sure, the women idea wasn't working too well, but much more important to Segura was his promotion to playing the main event with Kramer. These matches were the critical test of Pancho's game, and he knew it. Every match became a question of slaying the dragon, and every loss haunted him forever afterward.

"I lost a match to him in Santa Barbara. I had him 5–0, 5–1. I couldn't sleep that night. Jack was a tough competitor. He wanted to destroy you. He was a killer. I had the guy that time, and I lost 8–6 in the end. I was so upset, I had a sleepless night." Those were the matches that Pancho remembered afterward. "In London I had him 4–2 in the fifth set and still he beat me. I was still new as a headliner and he was the known star, and he thought I was not capable of playing that kind of tennis. He had size on me, big game, big overhead, his backhand was better than mine, but I moved very quickly, better than he did, and that surprised him. The only matches you hate to lose are those you are in a position of winning. It affected me for two or three days."

Pancho's competitiveness by now was a knife-edge drive, fueling his increasing aggressiveness on the court. It paid off. For the next three years, from 1951 through 1953, he crushed almost all his rivals in a dazzling series of wins. In early 1951 Frank Kovacs started well, winning the U.S. Pro Champs in Cleveland, Ohio, and the World Professional Champs in Lakewood, also in Ohio, but Segura came on strongly in the Canadian Pro championship, beating Kovacs 6–3, 10–12, 6–3, 6–3, before a large crowd at the Colosseum in Quebec City. Segura went on to win the most prized professional title, the U.S. Grass Court Pro Championship, at the West Side Tennis Club in Forest Hills, beating Gonzales 6–3, 6–4, 6–2 in an astonishing display of technical fireworks.

His double-handed forehand was now refined to an unbelievable, almost surgical, accuracy. Tony Trabert was to say that Segura "uses two hands like a croupier in Las Vegas." Added to this lethal weapon, his speed and anticipation on the court had become legendary. These skills, combined with his wicked tricks and witty antics playing to the bleachers, made him a wildly popular winner. At the end of 1951, Segura was rated number one in the PLTA (Professional Lawn Tennis Association) official rankings, over Gonzales, Riggs, and Kovacs.

In 1952, the Inca Warrior was unstoppable. After being defeated by Gonzales in the final of the British Pro Championship at Scarborough (toughing out a 15–13 first set before losing the next two), Segura took charge. He beat Kramer in a magnificent five-set match at Wembley, one of those matches that Segura would remember, not as a nightmare but as a moment of glory. Pancho lost the first two sets, 3–6, 3–6, and for a time it looked as though it would be yet another easy win for Big Jake over his long-time opponent. But Segura hunkered down and won the third set 6–2, the fourth set 6–4, and in a nail-biting fifth set forced Kramer to give up a 5–2 lead and a loss of his serve at 5-all after thirteen deuces, to pull out the victory, 7–5. According to Joe McCauley, in his book *The History of Professional Tennis*, Kramer was so upset at losing this match that he was reduced to tears afterward in the dressing room.

Pancho Segura was on a roll. He easily defeated Bobby Riggs (who continued to play in spite of having officially retired), for the U.S. Clay Court title in St. Augustine, Florida, and then went on to win the U.S. Pro title at Lakewood by beating Gonzales again in an excruciatingly long final. The last set was 6–0, a score that reflected the failing strength of the big Mexican-American, who was suffering from stomach flu. At the end of 1952 Segura was again ranked number one, over Gonzales, Kovacs, and Riggs.

In 1953, the character of the tour changed. Two new players

signed on—the world's number one amateur, Frank Sedgman, and his partner, Ken McGregor. Both Australian, these players brought new life to the tour, and fans came out to watch them stand up, *mano a mano*, against the favorites, Kramer and Segura. Kramer by this time was beginning to suffer from arthritis, and his play suffered, particularly against the new young champion, Sedgman. Kramer managed to win most of the matches, but it was a struggle.

Meanwhile, Segura was too quick and clever for McGregor, who found it a challenge to get any games at all off the wily Ecuadorian. Their final score in the spring tournament series was 71–25. In early July Segura traveled with the group to Caracas, Venezuela, where he won the Venezuela round-robin, defeating all three of his colleagues, Kramer, McGregor, and Sedgman.

Pancho again did brilliantly in England later that month, winning both British pro events. His finest matches were against McGregor, who was determined to ace the little Indian, but could not handle the smaller man's lightning speed, tenacity, and pinpoint accuracy (he lost in three sets), and against Sedgman, the new strong man, who was finally brought down in a fantastic show of fireworks in the final set, with Segura winning the match 2–6, 6–4, 3–6, 6–4, 8–6.

Segura, Gonzales, Pails, McGregor, and Sedgman packed in a grueling schedule for the rest of the year, playing in France, Italy, Belgium, Germany, Beverly Hills, Quebec, Long Island, Wembley, Germany again, and back to France for the final tournament of the year in November 1953, the Lyon Pro Champs, in which Segura beat Sedgman again in three sets, 3–6, 6–4, 6–3.

While Segura was striding through the tournaments like a conquistador, a shadow began to haunt his progress. At the end of 1953, perhaps the greatest of Segura's three great years on the tour, that shadow turned into a reality. Richard Gonzales had by now paid his dues as a runner-up and was about to claim the crown from his little compatriot. In 1954, Gonzales seized the limelight and never let it go.

For a long time now Gonzales had been known as Pancho. It

was an obvious name for him, after all. Like Segura, he was a Latino, dark-skinned, from a family born across the border. Didn't all gringos call people like that Pancho? Perhaps it was because gringos knew something about Pancho Villa, Mexico's great liberationist hero, and so lumped all Hispanics into the same category. So it was obvious to call him Pancho. But while Segura did not mind the name, Pancho Gonzales minded a lot. He thought it insulting. It epitomized for him the attitude whites had toward him and all Latinos. Beneath this condescending name he saw all sorts of hostility and mistrust.

He wasn't far wrong. The first year of Gonzales's disastrous pro tour, he was traveling in a car with his brother, Manuel, Segura, and Pails from a tournament in Dallas, where he had once again been dealt a crushing defeat by Jack Kramer. He had also just learned that his son Michael had been born. A celebration was in order. They picked up some beer and started the long trip to Shreveport, Louisiana, where they were to play next. A few miles outside Dallas, Big Pancho (once he arrived on the tour, he became "Big Pancho" and Segura "Little Pancho") wanted to make a pit stop at a small roadside diner. The four men went inside and decided to grab a bite to eat. The waitress ignored them. Unaware of the three white men sitting at the counter, Gonzales called out to her for service.

"We don't serve your kind here," drawled a deep Texas voice. Gonzales turned and stared. His brother grabbed his arm and urged him to stay calm. While Segura and Pails quickly scrambled to get out of the diner, Gonzales moved slowly, in his loping walk, toward the exit. One of the Texans stood in his way, and as he continued to move to the door, another one started calling out, "You colored wetback spics, go home to your greasy mamas." They laughed and went on jeering, "You spineless yellow-skinned wetbacks!" Gonzales could not take this. He turned on them and within seconds they were fighting viciously. Gonzales was hit hard and fell to the ground. "Get my gun," he yelled to Manuel, "it's in the car!"

Gonzales staggered out into the road toward the car, where the other three were huddled, staring anxiously out of the window. Suddenly an old black man appeared and told them to get out as quickly as possible. "They've hung people for what you've done," he warned them urgently. Furious, Gonzales got into the car and they drove away. "In those days, Mexicans weren't too welcome in Texas," Segura said later in a wry understatement. "We had to keep him from fighting. He had no fear. He'd challenge anybody."

That incident was only one in a year that humiliated Gonzales from start to finish. At a too-young age, he had turned professional in a fanfare of publicity, only to find he could not work with—or defeat—Jack Kramer. What was behind all these defeats was, of course, something else, something more insidious. Without anyone saying it, it was clear that Kramer's favorites were the big, white, attractive all-American players who had been playing with him over the years, such as Schroeder, Parker, Kovacs, and later Tony Trabert. They were the stars in Kramer's hierarchy and were treated accordingly, as were the glamorous Australians who joined the tour in the early fifties. Kramer would argue that his strategy was simply about squeezing money out of the increasingly unsuccessful tour.

In contrast, Richard Gonzales, treated as a nobody, was dropped from the tour at the end of 1950. To add to the insult of women being brought in to replace him on the court, he went home to Los Angeles to find his wife, Henrietta, now the mother of two boys, living in squalor, with the house full of soiled diapers and dirty dishes. Soon Big Pancho found himself trying to be a family man instead of a world-famous athlete, and he hated it. He was still only twenty-two years old.

He played with his dogs, gambled, tinkered with cars, became involved in drag racing. What had happened to his tennis? The newspapers were already saying—again—that he was washed up, a flash in the pan, a cheese champ. "The beating he had taken from Kramer had undoubtedly broken his spirit," columnist Arthur Marx wrote.

From 1951 to 1953, while Little Pancho was wowing audiences all over the world with his amusing shenanigans and brilliant tennis, Big Pancho played in a few limited events, winning some, losing some, trying to keep his game sharp. In 1952 he beat the legendary Bill Tilden 6–1, 6–2 in an American tour event, and later, at Wembley, he defeated Kramer in a dazzling display of tennis after being two sets down, 3–6, 3–6, 6–2, 6–4, 7–5. Nineteen fifty-three was another hard year, with Sedgman beating him in the French Pro Champs. Choosing not to travel to Europe that summer, he came back strongly at the California Pro Champs in Beverly Hills, where he won the title against Don Budge (5–7, 6–3, 6–4,), and at the Canadian Pro Champs, defeating Bobby Riggs in the final 6–0, 6–4, 6–4. Both these three-set victories were to pave the way for his victorious comeback in 1954.

In doing so, he had to unseat the current champion, his traveling companion and amigo, Pancho Segura.

"We had a friendship, a warm friendship," Little Pancho recalled. "It was like a brotherhood, since we were both Latin-American."

In those days, they were still outsiders, dark-skinned strangers on the court, noticeable for their ethnicity, in contrast to Kramer's favored stars. Little Pancho had learned to live with it, even enjoy it, playing to the minority fans, teasing the big boys, making the most of his Latin background. But Big Pancho was made of different stuff. His violent childhood, rebelliousness, and sensitivity to slights made him vulnerable. "Prior to the tour," he explained, "Kramer had set the tone for our relationship by his obvious dislike toward me. During the tour that dislike grew to hatred and I grew to hate him as much as he hated me. The hatred and anger inside of me emerged as a driving force that would eventually make me a dominating figure in professional tennis."

Big Pancho and Little Pancho traveled together on the tour for almost ten years. Little Pancho had first seen Gonzales play in 1944 at the Los Angeles Tennis Club. He was playing Herbie Flam. "I saw the guy play so well, so naturally, and with such a great serve. I recall a match where he was love–40 down and he made five aces in a row. I never saw anything like it. Five aces consecutively. I thought it was a fluke."

Segura soon learned it was not a fluke. "Gonzales was very gifted and a natural. Perhaps only Federer today has the same gifts." As the tour continued, Segura watched his friend get better and better at the game of tennis. He also watched him off the court, getting angrier and angrier at his treatment from the authorities. Untrained in the social niceties, Big Pancho found it hard to deal with the elitist culture of tennis. He was used to street life, gambling, smoking, drinking, living on the edge. People called him *pachuco*, a street kid. He resented the name, but it was not far from the truth. Now he was supposed to train, to care for his body, to avoid trouble, to talk politely, to wear suits, and show up at publicity events. He was never to accept fully any of these requirements.

"Pancho was just in way over his head," Jack Kramer wrote in his book, *The Game*. "On the court, Gorgo would swig Cokes through a match." (Kramer made sure there was always a cold Coke waiting for Gonzales, although he knew it was bad for the athlete—a piece of gamesmanship that did not go unnoticed by Gonzales's friends.) "He also had terrible sleeping habits, made even worse by the reality of a tour. He couldn't get to sleep after a match under the best conditions—and try getting to sleep every night when you're losing."

When Gonzales was invited to visit Europe after winning his big amateur titles in 1949, he was approached by an acquaintance called Neil McCarthy, who saw that the young Mexican-American needed help. McCarthy was an elderly attorney with a passion for tennis, and after he learned that Gonzales was going to France, Germany, and England, he decided he would take the street kid in hand. He took Gonzales shopping and bought him suits and shirts and evening clothes for the trip.

Like Segura, Gonzales attracted rich patrons who helped smooth the way for their inexperienced protégé into the glamorous world of celebrity sports. Neil McCarthy, like Arturo Cano for Segura, taught Gonzales some of the finer points of good behavior. Another such patron for Gonzales was Frank Shields (grandfather of actress Brooke Shields), who was a fine Davis Cup player, and well connected socially. Shields also took Gonzales under his wing when the Mexican-American was at the beginning of his career and tried to make him eat better, dress better, and gamble less in order to prepare himself for the arduous life of a professional tennis player.

There were other similarities between Segura and Gonzales. They both had strong, ambitious mothers who worshiped their eldest sons and wanted to see them succeed. They both came from large families, with never enough money to provide for them. They were both ferociously competitive and determined to improve their game to win every title in the book. They were both intelligent, although Gonzales never exercised his mind the way Segura did. "He was never curious about anything," Segura recalled. "He never wanted to know anything. I used to say to him, 'I'm not as big as you, or as smart as you, but you should buy *Time* magazine and see what's going on in the world.' And he'd say, 'What the hell do I need that for? I have you!'"

Little Pancho laughed uproariously at Richard's carefree responses, although he knew it had a destructive side. Particularly in his financial dealings with Jack Kramer, Gonzales was like a mad bull, charging again and again into Kramer's stonewalling tactics. Segura knew he couldn't help Gonzales in these battles, which became increasingly bitter, and damaged both men's careers. Gonzales called Kramer "Czar" Kramer, and fought to the end about his right to bigger percentages and better contracts. Kramer forced him to play places and make appearances that Gonzales felt were not contractually binding, and finally in 1960 he brought a lawsuit against the Czar. He won the arbitration, and with that Gonzales turned his back on Kramer for good. "He was a peculiar guy," Little Pancho said fondly of Gonzales. "He was a nice guy if he liked you. If he didn't like you, it didn't matter if you had money or power, he didn't give a damn."

The two Panchos liked and admired each other, both on and off the court. Segura was seven years older than Gonzales, and he tried to look after the younger man. "Pancho Segura and I shared a camaraderie," Gonzales said. He only once got angry at Segura, after Segura beat him in the early days. "It was 1951, in Bogota, Colombia. Gorgo said he would beat me up. I made him look bad. But that didn't last long." As the two got to know each other better, they played good tennis against each other, keeping the scores mostly even.

They also paired up at times against the gringos. One of Kramer's tour routines involved a seeding system, reevaluated every ten matches, which kept the players on their toes. If there were four players going out to play, the first seed played the fourth seed and the second seed played the third. The two winners then played each other. The man seeded fourth had the hardest draw, playing the first seed on the first night, meaning extra work on the court. The players called this position "the cellar," and they worked mightily to avoid being there.

Gonzales and Segura found cunning ways to stay out of the cellar. "He was a master at working angles. I enjoyed his manipulative escapades," Gonzales recalled. He gave the example of how Segoo managed to "psych" Gonzales to beat Sedgman, who was winning most of their matches. One night Big and Little Pancho were watching an Ice Follies performance in Philadelphia together, and they started talking about the Sedgman problem. "We gotta keep him in the cellar, Gorgo," Segura said. "He's too physically fit." Big Pancho asked what Segoo had in mind.

What Segoo had in mind was simple. Take Sedgman to the party being held later that night, make sure he had a few drinks, and leave him there. The plan worked like a charm. Sedgman stayed all night at the party and didn't recover for a week, meanwhile losing all his matches and staying permanently in the cellar. Gonzales appreciated that kind of strategy from his tennis amigo.

People who doubted the competitiveness of the tour greatly underestimated the players' desire to win. Little Pancho recalled one occasion on the Duel of the Decade tour when Bobby Riggs was sick and asked Jack to "carry" him, meaning, "Don't beat me too badly." Segura shook his head at the memory and laughed. "Jack beat the crap out of him. Jack was tough. If you beat him, he wouldn't talk to you for two or three days." Arriving at a new place, they always practiced to test the conditions of the court (which were usually extremely challenging), so they might find how best to win. "I'd always ask one of the guys to come and hit," Segura said. "They always would. Nobody wanted to lose."

Only Gonzales refused to play ball, so to speak. He often let his weight balloon up, he would stay out late, he would not show up. When someone asked Gonzales who he was playing the next day, he would sometimes say, "I'm having a routine match." If his opponent heard this, he would turn on him in fury. *A routine match!* And yet he famously hated to lose. Several players remembered occasions when they beat Gorgo and he would not speak to them for weeks.

The better Gonzales became at tennis, the more unreliable he became. He knew he was a star, and behaved like one. He would explode on the court, like John McEnroe twenty years later. He frequently threw his racket on the ground. He would shout at linesmen, "You need a Seeing Eye dog!" Or, "When was the last time you saw an eye doctor?" People began to expect fireworks from the big guy, and they usually got it. "He got mad but he was funny, he made them laugh," Segura said. "He created excitement, you know, because in those days tennis was very quiet. You couldn't talk." Like Segura, with his self-encouragement, "*Ahora, Pancho, ahora! Vamos!*" Gonzales made a lot of noise on the court.

If he created excitement, he also aroused anger. One time the group was in Paris, about to fly to Copenhagen, where they were to play on the weekend, when they would get a bigger draw. "Gonzales suddenly decided to go from Paris to Los Angeles on Sunday night," Segura remembered, "then fly on Thursday to Copenhagen." The idea was perfectly ridiculous. "The promoter in Copenhagen is dying because Gonzales is the marquee name, and we are all dying because we need him there for the publicity and practice. He'd annoy us like that." In the end he showed up, but this was not the first or the last time he played games with his tour mates, and they did not like it.

Even his only real friend and supporter, Little Pancho, was not immune to Gonzales's erratic behavior. After they had both left the tour, they were due to play doubles together in an over-forty-five tournament at Wimbledon. But Big Pancho got upset about something and took off to California. "He dropped me. I had to default." But big-hearted Segura could not really be angry. "He was a peculiar guy," he repeated, shrugging.

They used to go out together in the evenings, but Gonzales was difficult to please, often ignoring the women who consistently threw themselves at him. Little Pancho laughed and confessed he got sick of going out with him, since Gonzales was always the *tesoro*, the target of all the females. "We shared everything except women," Segura said.

The dark-eyed, dark-skinned, six-foot-three tennis god, with the mysterious scar and the sensuous pantherlike body, was a magnet to the opposite sex. "He could have been a movie star," Segura said. "I remember Jack Warner sending an agent to get him to sign a contract. They were going to train him, teach him how to walk, how to handle a knife and fork. But he said no. He didn't like it. He said there were too many sissies in the movie business."

On one occasion, when the two Panchos were in Rome, the granddaughter of the king of Italy took an interest in Gonzales. "She spoke in Spanish to me about him and said she wanted to give us a party." Segura recalled. "When I told Gonzales he swore at me and said he didn't want to go out with such an ugly female. I couldn't believe it! I tell you, he was mean with women. Women were his downfall."

Women *were* his downfall. Segura knew what he was talking about. He had seen Gonzales fall for the wrong women at the wrong time. He knew about his troubles with his first wife, Henrietta, his divorce and marriage to a former Miss Rheingold, Madelyn Darrow. She aspired to a higher social elevation than her husband's (including changing the spelling of Gonzales back to a "z" because that's how it was spelled in Castilian Spanish). They divorced and then briefly remarried. Segoo sighed over his friend's passion for a dental assistant whom he impulsively married and then abandoned with their baby in a hotel room in London while he played at Wimbledon.

Big Pancho's last marriage was to Rita Agassi, the sister of another great tennis player, Andre Agassi. Gonzales had coached Rita when she was a lovesick thirteen-year-old at Caesar's Palace in Las Vegas. After living together for three years, they married in 1984. He was fifty-five, and she was twenty-three. They had a son, Skylar, and divorced after ten years. In all, Richard Gonzales had six marriages and eight children. Segura once joked that the nicest thing Gorgo ever said to his wives was, "Shut up."

"He was a loner," Segura said. "He would go out at night alone. He liked tinkering with cars and would drive off into the mountains for hours. Or go hunting by himself." Cliff Perlman, former owner of Caesar's Palace in Las Vegas, said the same thing. In the 1960s, when Gonzales was running the tennis program there, Perlman would watch him go off in some car he had been working on. "He'd get into his car and drive to Phoenix and back—alone."

If the lone wolf had a friend in this cutthroat world, it was Pancho Segura. "Segura is like a very close older brother to me," Gonzales once told author Joel Drucker. "He has such energy and love for life that I would listen to him talk about anything—tennis, events, politics, poverty. He seemed aware of the world at a young age."

As the 1950s progressed, Gonzales began to beat Segura on a regular basis. No longer was Segura the top-ranked pro in the world, or even in the United States. Richard Gonzales claimed those titles for himself, and he earned them. In 1954 for the first time Gonzales won the World Championship number one ranking. In Mexico and later in the U.S. pro Hard Court Championships, Gonzales twice beat Segura (the second a tough five-setter).

In August of that year, Segura fought back to gain number one in the final standings at the Pacific Coast Pro Champs in Beverly Hills. In October Gonzales beat Kramer twice, in Manila and in Hong Kong, and at the end of 1954, he won the Australian pro series over Sedgman and Segura. From then on, Gonzales totally dominated the game until 1962.

In fact, although historians still tend to rate Jack Kramer as the top player from 1951 to 1953, the record shows, as tennis writer David Hernandez points out, that Gonzales was winning most of his matches from 1951 onward. Marshalling statistics of Gonzales's winning record over his astonishingly long career, Hernandez goes on to claim that Gonzales was the greatest tennis player of all time—"By far!"

Segura did not let "the greatest tennis player of all time" get off lightly. He was too competitive for that. Friendship never got in the way of the desire to win. Jack Kramer describes an unforgettable match in March 1955, when Segoo played Gorgo for the World Pro Champs title in Cleveland, Ohio. The match was complicated by the fact that it was the first VASS tournament (Van Alen Simplified Scoring System), whereby games were played to twenty-one, and you had to win by two. But the most important new rule was that you only got one serve. Jack March, the promoter, along with Jimmy Van Alen, a rich tennis patron from Newport who often thought up ways to tinker with the game, thought it would eliminate the (sometimes boring) domination of the big serve. It was a plan that played directly against Gonzales's strength, and he was furious at it. (Gonzales had already had a screaming confrontation with Van Alen on the tennis court at Newport, where Van Alen reigned as king.)

To prove them all wrong, Gonzales played like a genius and got to the final—against Segura. It was a brutal seesaw of a match. Segura took it to a final set after losing the first 16–21, winning the second, 21–19, losing the third, 8–21, and winning the fourth 22–20. In the fifth set, Gonzales was up 20–8, with eleven match points in his pocket. As Kramer conceded, at that time Gonzales was the best player in the world, and most people watching thought the final was over. But Gorgo grew confident, and sneaky Segoo dug down deeper and deeper, fending off that tantalizing match point over and over again by running off seven straight points. The score went to 15–20, with Segura serving. Gonzales, rattled, decided to change his rackets for one that had tighter strings to block serves with more impact.

"And now Segoo really went wild." Kramer wrote, "Everything he hit was a winner. At 18–20, he played the most fantastic point I ever saw, lobbing the ball way up into the arena overhead lights, somehow guiding it safely between them like it was a missile." Gonzales managed to return the lob, then Segura sent up another, again missing all the lighting, wires, and pipes in the ceiling. Gonzales could not keep going under this relentless barrage of pinpoint accuracy. Segura pulled up to 19–20, with the little guy to serve. "The crowd was going wild. I have never seen Gonzales look so scared," Kramer said.

All Segura had to do now, having played inspired tennis to almost draw level, was to call up one of his most reliable serves and tie it up. "Segura threw the ball up, brought the racket forward, met the ball and sent it—plop, right into the net. There was dead silence in the arena. Suddenly it was Gonzales who remembered the one-serve rule. He leaped up into the air and dashed up to the net. He had won!"

The one-serve rule did not last long. But it had lasted long enough to give Pancho Segura nightmares for the rest of his life. In 1956 an almost equally grueling match for the title resulted in another win for Gonzales, and again in 1957. The tide was turning.

These kinds of gut-wrenching duels between the two Latino stars were played out many nights around the world, to the fans' delight. Sometimes they played doubles together, which the fans also loved—the two colorful Latinos, one tall, one short, against the big, white-skinned gringos. But for the two of them, the singles matches brought out the best in their temperaments and talents, the huge big-serving Gorgo against the little speed artist, Segoo—a perfect matchup.

"Oh, (Segura) beat me plenty of times all right," Gonzales told writer Joel Drucker. "He could be real trouble if I was just a bit off."

In conversations with Drucker, Gonzales and Segura relived a memorable match in Sydney, Australia, in 1957, that Drucker later described:

Down two sets to love in his quarterfinal versus Australian Rex Hartwig, Segura heeded Gonzales's advice to put on spikes to gain better footing. Playing brilliantly, Segura fought back to win, but his wrist was throbbing. Gonzales helped out, massaging his friend's wrist, getting him treatment from a trainer in advance of Segura's next match—a semi-final against Gonzales.

The next day, on the fast grass court that had bedeviled Segura back in 1940, Gonzales sprinted off to a big lead, taking the first two sets. But again Segura dug in, winning the last three sets.

"Boy, I was ticked," said Gonzales, laughing. "I'd helped him recuperate and then he beat me."

The next day Segura whipped Australian Frank Sedgman in three straight sets. But it's the win over Gonzales that he cherished the most.

"Gonzales is the player that I would have played for my life," says Segura. "It's that simple."

So as in the great human dramas of history, the younger man finally gains the skills to defeat the master. But even as their fates changed, Jack Kramer knew that Segura would always have a permanent place in the hearts of the fans. "Even without the titles, Pancho got the recognition. There was always the feeling that people would go home and say, 'Wasn't Gonzales's serve terrific?' and 'You've got to give Kramer credit. He slowed him down and beat him. But goddammit, Segura was the guy that made the evening for me.'"

Pancho Segura made the evening for thousands of tennis lovers during those years. But like Gonzales, he was finding life back home more and more difficult. "It's not a normal life," Segura said. "You can't have a relationship with anyone because you are on the road all the time. I loved the game too much to make time for women. The wives suffered. I'd tell a player today not to marry until he has stopped playing tennis professionally." While Gonzales went from victory to victory, his women fell by the wayside. For Segura, the years on tour took their inevitable toll, and by the end of the 1950s he had to face a new set of challenges that would involve a great deal more than lobbing a perfect ball into the skylights.

Chapter Eight Playing Hard, Playing Tough

On July 9, 1952, Virginia gave birth to a son, Spencer Francisco Segura. Pancho was not home. He was, as usual, away on tour.

At first, Virginia had eagerly traveled on the tennis circuit with her husband, but after those first exciting years, she had begun to find the schedule difficult and exhausting. During the early part of their marriage, when Pancho was away, Virginia stayed with her mother, and when he came back, they rented small furnished apartments in New York. "Some great dumps," Virginia remembered, laughing. "I tried to find inexpensive places. Pancho would have stayed in some tennis players' hotel, but I wanted to save for a house. Once we rented rooms in an apartment that belonged to what was then called a taxi dancer. She was from Lithuania and had obviously been through hard times."

Spencer was born in New York, on one of the hottest days of the year. "I was renting a place in Rego Park," Virginia said, "but Pancho wanted to move to Southern California, where all the good tennis—and weather—was, so after three months, with Spencer in good shape, I decided to leave New York and find a place for us in Los Angeles." Virginia left the baby with her mother and a family maid and went to California. She stayed there in a rented apartment and began house hunting. The days turned into weeks. Finally, she got a call from her mother, who was desperate. "Virginia," she cried. "Come home! I can't do this!" Virginia had been away almost two and a half months.

Fortunately, Pancho was about to come back to New York after a European tour, and so he picked up Spencer (meeting him for the first time) from Virginia's mother and took him on a plane to Los Angeles, where Virginia had found them a pleasant little apartment in Culver City. "It was a good time at first," Virginia remembered. "I would take the baby on tour. We went to Australia when Spencer was two. I remember I got scratched by a koala bear. But it was difficult traveling to so many different places with a two-year-old and no help. After a while Spencer got sick, and the doctor told me he should stay home. So after that we didn't tour so much."

The Seguras managed to find the money to buy a house on Holmby Avenue in West Los Angeles. It was in terrible shape, but it was all they could afford. Pancho settled them in and then took off again. Little Spencer soon learned what it meant to have a father on the road all the time. At first, he and his mother went along—as far as Australia, which was quite a long distance when air travel was in its infancy. By the age of four, he had been to Europe at least twice. He was often the only child on the tour. The other players mostly left their children at home, because they were older and in school, or for other reasons. "But then my mother said I couldn't go along anymore, and then it became difficult for us both."

Even at that young age, Spencer sensed how lonely his mother was at home, and how sad she was that Pancho was away so much. "He was gone for such huge stretches of time. And then he would come back, and everything would be fantastic. The dog would come out from under the bed, and my mother would be smiling. And then he would go away again. It was a terrible sort of existence, you're waiting for your father and then he'd arrive and everything would be exciting and then all of a sudden he'd have to leave again." Spencer, like all small children with absent fathers, suffered tremendously from these separations. "Going to the LAX airport with my Dad was a very depressing thing for me, because we'd be saying good-bye again and my mother would be crying in the car."

Pancho made his living as a professional tennis player. To pay the bills, he had to play tennis as much and as often as possible, wherever in the world the tour took him. Even with his winning record and his huge popularity with audiences, these successes did not translate into more money. Throughout his pro career, the question of money was in the forefront of his mind, and that meant playing tennis. Like an actor, he had to perform to stay alive. He was a driven man.

Not only did he now have to support a wife and child, but he was already beginning his lifetime's commitment to helping his own family back in Ecuador. As early as 1945, he had arranged for his eldest sister, Elvira, to come to the United States to work for Arturo Cano, Pancho's patron. Quick and intelligent, she soon got another job making gramophone needles for the RCA Victor Company. She was also beautiful, and Pancho was determined that she stay in the United States. He had seen how the boys admired her back home, and he put his foot down. "No Latin lovers for my sister," he announced. He told his mother that Ecuador, with its backward culture of women being regarded as either saints or whores, was no place for intelligent young women, and although his mother wept she knew he was right. Elvira married Albert Karam, whom she had met in New York, the same year that Pancho married Virginia. It was a long, successful, and happy marriage. "Pancho did so much for me. I am so grateful," she said.

Pancho also worked to bring his other sisters to America and helped pay their way. All of them finally left Ecuador. But his generosity touched more people than his immediate family. "He brought me here to the U.S. in 1951," his first cousin Carmita Zafman said. "I needed a sponsor and Pancho found one for me. When I was first in New York, I lived with Virginia for a while. The first time I went back to Ecuador was in 1959." Carmita married a doctor and lives in California. "Whatever I am I am because of him," she declared.

Pancho himself felt frustrated at being unable to do more. "I could not send them all to school," he said.

Until he was eight, Spencer hardly saw his father. Pancho would come back on his lightning visits and bring presents, toys from all over the world. The local kids would come and admire them. But it didn't really make up for the absences. Spencer knew he was different. At school, his friends' fathers were always around. "We were like a little island, my mother and I," he recalled. "She wasn't particularly social. Everything was about waiting for him to come home."

But Pancho couldn't come home. He had another tournament, another match, in Canada, or Germany, or Sweden, or Peru. He had to keep his position on the tour, and it was getting more difficult all the time. New talent kept coming in to keep the old guard on their toes. In 1955 Jack Kramer brought in Tony Trabert, who had just won both Wimbledon and Forest Hills. Kramer thought Gorgo versus Trabert would be a good matchup, but the promoters, who continued to be wary of the tempestuous Gonzales, urged Kramer to continue to headline the tour. Gonzales was very annoyed at this slight. Kramer knew his playing days were numbered, so he ignored the promoters and signed the fiery Mexican-American to a seven-year contract, giving him 20 percent. "He made fifty-six thousand dollars that first year," Kramer said, "beating Trabert almost as badly as I had once beaten Gonzales." (These defeats did not sit well with Trabert, who found Gonzales as offensive an individual as Kramer had.)

The other two star amateur players Kramer had his eye on were Lew Hoad and Ken Rosewall, a pair of gifted Australians who were winning big matches, including the 1954 Davis Cup against Trabert and Kramer. In 1953, at the age of nineteen, Rosewall had won the Australian and French singles and the Wimbledon doubles. Hoad, the same age as Rosewall, won the Wimbledon doubles with Rosewall, and in 1954 carried off the Australian doubles, along with the French doubles and mixed doubles titles. Originally agreeing to turn pro in 1955, they both reneged, in spite of large contracts.

Rosewall then signed for sixty-seven thousand dollars in 1956 and entered into a long-running duel with Gonzales, made more interesting by their strikingly different styles of play on the court.

While Gonzales typically threw his huge and imposing weight about with linesmen and umpires, Rosewall was always quiet and contained. In the end, Gonzales won the 1956 series against the young Australian by 50-26. But the big draw was the handsome blonde hunk, Hoad, who finally signed in late 1957 for one hundred thousand dollars. These two Australians invigorated the tour and brought Australian fans to the pro game.

Pancho was thirty-seven years old in 1958, when the two Australians presented their fireworks displays of tennis to the world. Kramer still relied greatly on Segura, not only for his colorful personality to bring in the fans but to provide exciting matches, which he did, beating Rosewall consistently with his merciless attacks on the young Australian's weak forehand. The style of speedy little Rosewall was compared by some aficionados to Segura's in his anticipation and lightning court coverage. Ellsworth Vines once asked Rosewall who he thought was the greatest small man of the modern era, Segura or Rosewall. "Segura," Rosewall replied. "No doubt about it. When I joined the pros he beat me for over a year."

The big matchup everyone was looking for was Hoad versus Gonzales, and throughout 1958 the two men battled it out in front of sellout crowds in Australia, New Zealand, Europe, and the United States, with Rosewall and Segura following closely behind. If Gonzales finally managed to win most of the contests against Hoad, it wasn't until after some of the most brutally fought matches anyone had ever seen.

Nineteen fifty-eight was an important year for Little Pancho. His opponents were getting younger and stronger. His own skills had to be supplemented more and more by shrewd mental strategy and iron willpower. He did well the first part of the season, coming in third in the Melbourne Round-Robin. He was defeated by Gonzales in two sets in the World Pro Champs in Cleveland (Gonzales went on to win, beating Hoad 3–6, 4–6, 14–12, 6–1, 6–4).

In the Tournament of Champions at Forest Hills in June, Segura came in fifth, behind Gonzales (the winner), Rosewall, Trabert, and Hoad. But in the Masters Round-Robin in Los Angeles in July, Segura pulled out a brilliant series of victories, beating Gonzales, Hoad, Trabert, and Rosewall, to end up number one in the final standings. After a grueling sixteen-stop tour of France in September for the Perrier Trophy, Segura came in second behind Rosewall, and in the final tournament of the year in Vienna, Austria, he beat Trabert in three sets for the championship. At the end of the year, promoter Jack March's end-of-year rankings put Gonzales at number one, Hoad at number two, and Segura at number three, above Trabert, Rosewall, and Sedgman. At thirty-eight years old, that was a pretty remarkable statistic for the Inca Warrior.

But it did not mean that he could stop, take a rest, go home for a while. Although Kramer was giving big money to his new stars, Segura never could bring up his salary to anything like the amount he needed. He had to stay on the tour. And the tour was not getting any easier.

Jennifer Hoad married Lew in 1955 and joined the tour with him when he turned pro in 1957. "Jack Kramer organized a one-hundred-match series for Lew against Gonzales in Australia," she said. "I went with him then, but mostly I stayed home. I had two children by that time, and when the kids could be looked after I'd leave for two weeks or so. But Virginia stuck with the whole tour, and it was very hard for her. One of the problems was Pancho not driving. He always got lost! They'd always arrive last at our next destination. I don't know how she coped."

Pancho's driving—or lack of it—became one of the big jokes on the tour. "He told us all he couldn't drive," Tony Trabert said. "And then when we would be driving, he'd be sleeping in the car, resting up for his matches." "Sure I knew how to drive," Segura sighed. "But not very well. Besides, why did I want to use up all my energy behind the wheel?" (He was not called "Sneaky" for nothing.) On one occasion Lew Hoad put him behind the wheel in Tallahassee to complete the drive to Tampa. Lew then went to sleep, only to wake up still in Tallahassee! Pancho told him he couldn't find his way out.

The long journeys were trying for everybody. "The boys always wanted to push on to the next city," Jenny Hoad remembered, "and the women wanted to stop. The wives would get very bored. They'd have to go to the stadium and watch two singles and doubles each night, often going to five sets, and then they had to wait while their husbands showered and changed, so they were always waiting, getting more and more hungry and exhausted. You had to be very, very patient." Afterward, they might get four hours' sleep if they were lucky, before moving on to the next stop.

There was often tension, and Jenny Hoad, like so many others, found Richard Gonzales the most difficult player to get along with. "He was very solitary, and very moody. He was like an angry cat. He didn't want people in the car with him. And of course he was very menacing on the court." The only person he accepted, she said, was Pancho Segura. Segoo's friendship with Gonzales made a huge difference, and they were all grateful that Little Pancho could handle Big Pancho's sulks and rages so well. Even when Gonzales drove off on his own, staying in a different motel, keeping himself apart, Segura would manage to coax him back on to the team.

"Segura was a bit of a clown," Jenny Hoad said, "and he would amuse everybody, defusing tension. He was so outgoing compared to Gonzales, so easygoing and independent. He always said what he thought. I remember once we were in Russia, and he kept making fun of the police and the guides, making wicked comments about Communism. 'I'm telling the truth, buddy,' he would tell them. It's a wonder he didn't get arrested!"

She also recognized Segura's tenacity and intelligence on the court, especially at that time when most of his opponents were at least ten years younger than he was. She said Lew had told her he learned more about tennis from Segura than from anyone else. "Segura was a wonderful competitor. Lew said that if you miss your first serve, don't bother with the second—Segura will always win on the return!"

Jack Kramer continued to make the tour rules, however arduous, and if you crossed him, you paid for it. Gonzales found that to his cost, and by the end of the decade he was out of the tour. Segura could not afford grandstanding like Gonzales did; he had to accept what he was given, and it was increasingly tough. "You weren't allowed to be sick," Jenny Hoad said. "Lew got thinner and thinner. He'd be gone half the year. There was never a day off. I can't imagine anyone doing it today. Now they are all paid millions, stay in the best hotels, make fortunes from advertising endorsements, and have their own chauffeurs to drive them everywhere. In those days it was motels if you were lucky. You had to drive yourself, and if you got snowed in you had to dig yourself out!"

The year 1959 was the beginning of the end for Jack Kramer as a tennis promoter. In spite of his best efforts, professional tennis had still not acquired the audiences he felt it deserved. "As the 1950s wore on, with no new American stars, the whole sport failed, amateur and pro together," Kramer said. "For the Davis Cup in 1954 at White City Stadium in Sydney, great temporary stands had to be constructed and there was a turn-away crowd of twenty-eight thousand. A decade later, the Aussies could not come close to selling the twelve thousand permanent seats."

In 1959, Kramer signed up Ashley Cooper and Mal Anderson, both Australians with the handsome, white-boy looks that Kramer felt the tour required. Cooper in particular had movie-star quality and was a big draw, having won the Australian singles and doubles, the Wimbledon singles, and the U.S. singles a year earlier. (Only the French eluded his bid for the Grand Slam.) Kramer started a big tour of Australia to showcase his new players, and it was reasonably successful, although Gonzales played his usual flamboyant and argumentative role in his matches. When Segura beat Rosewall and Hoad in Melbourne, Lew joked that the Aussies were furious at Segoo's trouncing the local boys—he was ruining the gate! Hoad won the series, with Gonzales coming in fourth, to his chagrin.

Gonzales did not let that statistic stand for long. For the rest of the year he played masterfully, until continuing disputes with Kramer caused him to refuse to play two of the biggest matches of the pro tour, Paris and Wembley. At Wembley, Segura found his familiar form and beat Hoad in three sets. On a roll, he then defeated Trabert and found himself in the final against Mal Anderson, whose pro career so far had not been distinguished. On this occasion Anderson played his best tennis, and the experienced Ecuadorian had to work hard. Segura reached match point in the fifth set at 5–4, but Anderson held him off and after returning the favor by fighting off Segura with three match points himself, Anderson won the set and the match 8–6.

Segura continued to do well, and in the South African tour he came second to Rosewall in the final standings. There was an irony to Pancho's attendance at the South African tournaments. Kramer had refused to take the tour to South Africa in earlier years, because "they wouldn't give Segoo the same visa as the white-skinned players." John Hall, a member of Gene Mayer's tennis academy, was a boy in South Africa during that '59 visit. When the tour came to Johannesburg, his father, William, a keen tennis aficionado, took him to see the pros play. John recalled that Pancho was not allowed to enter a nightclub with the others after the match, until his father made such a scene that they let him in.

Little Pancho, neither then nor at any time, ever complained about racial discrimination. Vic Braden, founder of the Vic Braden Tennis College, who worked on the tour briefly with Kramer before becoming a professional psychologist, said that even though he must have been subjected to it, "Segura was so good at ingratiating himself with people that they loved him right away. He caused people to be color blind." How different from Big Pancho, who was haunted by race issues throughout his life. When Arthur Ashe said in his book *Days of Grace* that it was not AIDS but being black that was the greatest burden he had to bear, Gonzales said he felt the same. Six months before he died, he told his brother Ralph that he should have taken the offer of the Mexican government in 1948 to give up his U.S. citizenship and play for Mexico. His bitterness at how he had been treated by his American "WASP" colleagues on the tour stayed with him all his life.

At the end of 1959, Kramer and the French newspaper *L'Equipe* agreed to give Segura the number six ranking, with Gonzales at number one, Sedgman at number two, and Rosewall at number three. In 1960, Gonzales continued to hold the top spot, but the feud with Kramer was reaching its climax, and Gonzales refused to play the Australian Indoor Champs in May. Instead, he accepted an invitation from a rival promoter, Jack Evans, to play in the Tuscaloosa Pro Champs. Kramer, furious, said he would sue him, but Gonzales played anyway, and won. The rift between the two men was now too great for reconciliation, and after chalking up some impressive victories for Kramer in the United States, Europe, and Australia, Gonzales, again the World Pro Champion, announced he would no longer play tennis on the tour.

Kramer had signed another young player, Alex Olmedo, who had represented the United States in the Davis Cup in 1958 and 1959 and had won both the Wimbledon and Australian singles in 1959. A Peruvian by birth, he was an attractive new talent, and Kramer hoped he would bring much-needed sexiness and excitement to the tour. Olmedo won an important Qantas round-robin match in Melbourne, defeating Sedgman 11–9, 6–1, but he was overshadowed by the devastating trio of Hoad, Rosewall, and Segura.

They called Olmedo "the Chief." He had put out the story that back in Peru he was an Indian chief and people paid him in gold to play tennis in the United States. He was astonished when people believed him. ("What ignorance!") Like Segura, he had arrived speaking hardly a word of English, with friends back home collecting money to send him to Miami. For the two men, it was a South American reunion. Segura and Olmedo had met in 1951 and again in 1954 when Olmedo was playing in junior tournaments in California as a tourist. When Olmedo ran into visa trouble, and was about to be sent back to Peru, Segura came to his rescue and arranged for him to go to Mexico and get his papers changed.

When Olmedo turned professional, Segura taught him the tricks of the tour. Nothing much had improved since Segura first joined. There was still a truck with a wood-and-canvas court that was laid over whatever surface they had been assigned. In Boston one time, Olmedo remembered having to wait to play until the Boston Celtics had finished their game.

Segura showed Olmedo how to work the court. "He was such an entertainer," the Peruvian remembered. "Audiences loved to side with him against the big guys. He had the best forehand I'd ever seen. He'd turn you into a windshield wiper on the baseline, then disguise a drop shot and kill you."

For Olmedo, the tour turned out to be a disaster. He had only played professionally for a few months before he began chalking up losses. He was simply not experienced enough to handle these defeats, and like Gonzales so many years earlier, he sank into a mood verging on despair. "The Chief knew it would be tough," Kramer observed, "but nothing in the world prepares you for losing day in and day out, and surely it is a hundred times worse to be losing every time when just last week you were the champion. It tears you apart. It did Olmedo."

Vic Braden was fascinated by the question of defeat and found Olmedo's example very telling. "He was considered one of the best players in the world, and coming off his tremendous Davis Cup triumph, he was a national tennis hero," Braden wrote in his book *Mental Tennis*. "In the pros, he lost by my count nineteen straight matches. Nineteen consecutive nights, Gonzales and the others murdered him." Braden attributed the problem to the way pro tennis worked in those days. "Alex was a great champion, but he was up against greater champions, Rosewall, Pancho Segura, and Gonzales, night after night. He did not have the opportunity he would today of playing in a field of sixty-four, a different tournament week after week. He would have flourished in such a professional system and become a multimillionaire. Instead, it was as if he had to play against Connors, Courier, and Edberg, each in his prime, night after night."

Olmedo quit the tour in 1965 and became a popular and highly successful coach at the Beverly Hills Hotel. "I had two kids, and at the hotel I could make more money and spend my time at home," he explained simply. Braden admired Olmedo for his decision. "To his credit, he was able to face this totally surprising defeat. He realized that while he would never be the champion he was before, it was not the end of the world. . . . A delightful man, he was able to keep this sudden turn in perspective." In an interesting aside, Jack Kramer reckoned that only three players turned out to be better pros than they were amateurs—Segura, Gonzales, and Rosewall.

The pro tour continued to struggle to cover costs. Kramer knew that what he was offering at this time was not appealing to players. The work was killing and the pay was pathetic. He could not make money for himself, let alone offer good deals. As he desperately brought in new faces (including Barry Mackay, Luis Ayala, Andres Gimeno, Robert Haillet, Kurt Nielson, and Mike Davies), he saw only empty seats. In 1960, the U.S. Grass Court Championships at Forest Hills were cancelled because of poor attendance.

The amateur tennis scene was equally dismal. By the end of the 1950s, the French, Australian, British, and U.S. championships could hardly get their stadiums half-filled. No television network had the slightest interest in covering the sport, not even the U.S. Championship at Forest Hills. Kramer was not only losing money but he was also being blamed for the problems of amateur tennis. He was accused of stealing all the good players from the amateur game and crippling its financial future, as well as excluding them from Davis Cup play. In 1961, the newly founded International Tennis Players Association introduced a new pro team cup, similar to—and competing with—the Davis Cup, hoping to attract new audiences and make money. It was to be called the Kramer Cup. This added insult to injury.

In 1961, the Australian officials were so angry at Kramer that they refused to allow him the use of their courts for his tournaments. During this crisis in the sport, the International Lawn Tennis Federation organized a vote to consider introducing open tennis. It was defeated by a small margin. The issue was not to be on the table again until 1968.

"The game was dull, and Gonzales, our champion, remained as

dominant and uncooperative as ever." Kramer was disillusioned. Segura sensed it. "We missed the boat, Kramer and I," he said. "We should have had a contract with a manufacturer making rackets and balls with our name on them, like they do now. Tennis was so small in those days." Segura also felt that the star system Kramer insisted on was unfair and that he never believed in the pro game. "You're wrong, Segoo," Kramer said. "We tried everything. The fans made it that way. They only wanted to see the stars. If they wanted a tournament, they'd go see the amateurs. It wasn't the way I wanted it, kid, it was the only choice I had."

In 1960, Pancho's marriage ended. The constant traveling and the inability to sustain a stable home life took their toll. Jenny Hoad had always found them an "odd combo," as she described them. "He was such an extrovert, and she was so cool and elegant. I used to think of that show, *The Prince and the Showgirl*, only they were the other way round—The Princess and the Showman."

There was also the inevitable temptation offered to all athletes on the road. "Of course there were other women," Virginia said evenly, "he was Latin-American." But Pancho was more careful than most; he never forgot Gardnar Mulloy's compelling advice about the cost in physical terms of spending a night with a woman. "I didn't want be tired all the time, running on to the court with my tongue hanging out!"

The divorce was difficult for both sides. But there was no going back. Eleven days after the divorce in 1961, Virginia remarried a very different kind of man, Edmund Giesbert, a distinguished entomologist and part-time actor. And Pancho, never one to waste time, had also found a new love, a beautiful divorcee called Beverley Young, who was to become his wife in a marriage celebrated almost as rapidly as Virginia had celebrated hers.

At the beginning of the new decade, Segura's disillusion with the financial side of the pro tour, his changed marital status, his cold-eyed assessment of his tennis game, all pointed to the same conclusion. It was time to quit.

In September 1962, Pancho Segura played the London Indoor

Pro Champs tournament on the hard wooden floor of Wembley Stadium. In the semifinal he was up against Ken Rosewall. The match was arduous and fiercely fought, both men small, fast, tenacious, and competitive. It went to five sets. "I had chances of winning it," Pancho said. But it was Rosewall's victory. The final score was 6–3, 4–6, 3–6, 7–5, 6–4. "The little guy beat me." Pancho was then forty-two years old; Rosewall was twenty-nine. At the end of the match, Pancho said he was so exhausted he couldn't walk. "That's when I saw the light."

He went on to play three more tournaments, in Switzerland, Italy, and, perhaps fittingly, the Kramer Cup Final in Adelaide, Australia, where he and Olmedo, playing for South America, were defeated in the doubles by the Australian team, Hoad and Rosewall. That was it. The baton had been passed. At the end of that year it was announced that another up-and-coming young Australian, Rod Laver, would turn professional and join the tour in 1963. A legendary new star was about to dazzle the tennis world.

So when Mike Franks, a teenage tennis champion from Southern California who used to play with Pancho at the Beverly Wilshire Hotel in Los Angeles ("He'd run me to death"), and as a Davis Cup player saw him sometimes on the tour, asked Segura if he would be interested in becoming the coach at the Beverly Hills Tennis Club, Pancho realized that this was a chance in a lifetime.

The timing was perfect.

The poor *cholo* from Guayaquil was ready to say good-bye to the career that had made him famous, that had given him experiences that he could never have dreamed of when he first left Ecuador, and that would stay with him forever. He was about to discover new horizons, with a new wife, and a new career as a coach. In so doing, he was being catapulted into a world of characters who up until then had seemed as distant as those Grace Line ships that he had gazed at all those years ago as a boy—the movers and shakers of the Hollywood movie industry.

Chapter Nine Coach to the Stars

I n 1961, a year before Pancho gave up the tour, he married Beverley Moylan Young. They had known each other since the late 1950s. Beverley's former husband, Larry, was a Kerkhoff, one of the richest families in California. They had helped found the Los Angeles Tennis Club, and when the Pacific Southwest tournament was held every year there, Larry would invite the players to their home for lunch. That is how Beverley first met Pancho.

"Larry and I were having problems," the gray-eyed beauty recalled. "I went with some friends to Hawaii and came back early when Pancho was coming through Los Angeles. He was interested in a friend of mine, who was also married, and they used to meet at my house." As time went on, and they got to know each other, Pancho decided he liked Beverley better than her friend. "Along the way, my knowledge of tennis improved tremendously!" she added, laughing.

The relationship developed into something more. Virginia and Pancho's divorce finally came through, so Pancho was free to commit himself to Beverley—"Of all the women in the world, one with three kids," she said ruefully, shaking her head. Beverley came from money herself, and was one of the bluebloods of California. In falling for her, Pancho was once again entering the upper-class world he had so successfully conquered on the tennis court. "It was an attraction of opposites," Beverley admitted later. "He was a very attractive man."

Virginia had remarried, and Pancho, booked to play tournaments in South America, took Beverley and Spencer, now eight years old, with him on the tour, which took them to South America. Beverley met the Segura family in Guayaquil. Her own background had protected her from some of the realities of severe poverty, and she was distressed by the conditions there. (It didn't help that Pancho's mother was just as disapproving of his second gringa as she had been of the first.)

But like Virginia ten years earlier, Beverley loved the traveling, particularly being the only woman—and a very good-looking one—traveling with a group of young, handsome tennis players. "It was lots of fun," she said. "But primitive!" She remembered sleeping on straw mattresses, in horribly cold rooms, and staying in a hotel where there was only one towel, which had to be shared with all the players. "You go first with the towel," they would tell her chivalrously. When she told Eva Gabor this story, the Hungarian star exclaimed, "How vunderful!"

Pancho and Beverley wanted to get married, but as they were still on the tour, the necessary paperwork, such as birth certificates, never seemed to materialize. "We went from one city to the other trying to get married." Finally, after a tennis tournament in Russia, they arrived in Paris and after yet another disappointing trip to London, Beverley decided to entrust her only hat with her friend, Tony Trabert's wife, to take back to the United States. But then they went back to England and found they could finally tie the knot at the Ecuadorian embassy in London. "I had been traveling all over the world. I only had a little suit to get married in," Beverley said. The marriage took place in front of the Ecuadorian ambassador, with Pancho Gonzales, Barry Mackay, Butch Buchholz, the Traberts, and Alex Olmedo in attendance. Mrs. Trabert brought Beverley her hat from Paris. They had a wedding lunch at the Athenaeum Court, where all the tennis players were staying, and then later that evening Pancho played at Wembley. That was their wedding night. They snatched a few days in Venice afterward.

"I didn't tell my mother," Beverley said. "I wrote her a letter. But unfortunately, the story was in *Time* magazine, and my mother read it before she received my letter. It's a terrible thing to have your mother mad at you." Beverley's mother was unforgiving, and at the beginning she was very tough on Pancho, calling him "the dark cloud." "'The dark cloud is arriving,' she would say," Pancho recalled with relish.

In those early days of the marriage, it was not only Beverley's mother who was angry. Beverley's three children, like most children of divorce, deeply resented this dark Latino invader for breaking up their home. They had led a luxurious life with their wealthy father, living in a big house that Gregory Peck had owned, with French servants, going to private schools, and enjoying trips to Europe every year. With Pancho, things were very different.

But Pancho, ever the crowd pleaser, was not about to let this unhappy situation drag on. Over time, he won the hearts not only of Beverley's children but of her mother. He insisted on inviting Mrs. Moylan to dinner, in spite of her hostility. "She came, and by the end of the evening she was madly in love with him!" Beverley remembered. Over the dinner table, Pancho would deliver his naughty stories with his usual panache in his Spanish accent to his Victorian mother-in-law. Beverley would desperately try to stop him, but her mother would say, "Quit shushing him!" She loved his wicked jokes! Pancho's personality in the end was too much for them. "Now they are all my buddies." (Beverley commented that later her children regretted they had wasted so much time hating him when they were young.)

The person who perhaps was most unsettled by this change in Pancho's life was Spencer. "My parents didn't tell me they were getting divorced," Spencer said. "It broke in the papers, on the news. I was at a Catholic school, and everyone said I'd go to hell for having parents who divorced."

He had known his parents were not getting along. Sometimes Pancho would be banished from the house and have to stay in a nearby motel. "That was tough on me. I would go and spend all the time I could with my dad, and I'd hang out with him and Gonzales and Rosewall." Gonzales used to pick up Spencer by the scruff of his neck like a kitten. Spencer loved it. But like Gonzales, Spencer was unruly in school. He didn't understand where his father was all the time or why he had to go to a school where his parents' divorce made him more of an outcast than he already was.

A few months after they were married, Pancho and Beverley moved into an apartment in Beverly Hills. Pancho was still traveling on the tour and, as usual, was gone much of the time. It was very hard on his new wife. Beverley had to continue taking care of her children, most of the time on her own, meanwhile trying to persuade them to accept their strange new stepbrother, Spencer, without Pancho there to ease the transition. The pressure on them all was very stressful. Later, though, Spencer and his stepmother became good friends.

Things were not much easier when Spencer was with his mother. His new stepfather, Edmund Giesbert, had German ideas of discipline, and Spencer, who had lived a rather free life with his mother, being the man of the house, the king of the castle, the permanent stand-in for his absent father, suddenly found himself not only being displaced by this alarmingly authoritarian figure but being restricted by harsh new rules of behavior. One of Giesbert's first acts as stepfather was to get rid of Spencer's dog, a very hurtful act to inflict on anybody, especially to an eight-year-old child of a broken home. Pancho had loved the dog, and Spencer remembered whenever his father came home the dog, a rambunctious German shepherd–Labrador mix, would obey Pancho like nobody else. ("When Gonzales came, he hid under the table," Spencer added.)

The loss of the dog was only one element of a series of painful adjustments for the boy. Edmund Giesbert's mother (like all the mothers in Pancho's story) was not pleased about Virginia Segura—a divorcee with a child—entering her family. Spencer heard her say to her son, "How can you come here with a divorcee and a half-breed?" Spencer was sometimes made fun of for being "Mexican."

Who could he turn to for help in understanding these difficult issues? With his mother wishing to please his autocratic, intellectually rigorous stepfather, and a stepmother preoccupied with her own children in the constant absence of her new husband, Spencer became essentially homeless. But in a few short years, his father's new career was to change all that.

By the time Pancho Segura arrived at the Beverly Hills Tennis Club in late 1962, he had become one of the most experienced tennis players in the business. To leave the game he loved to play, in order to teach it, was a huge decision. In 1961, Beverley remembered Jack Kramer calling her into his office and saying, "You aren't going to make our boy quit playing tennis, are you?" But two years later, even Kramer saw that the moment had arrived. "It was the only thing he could do, if you remember the times," Kramer said later. "The young ones were coming in and he was still a damn good player, but he did the logical thing. He cashed in on his skills."

And what skills they were. "The great thing that Pancho has is not the ability to improve a backhand by saying, "'Get your racket back, bend your knees, watch the ball follow through,' you know, like all the coaches," Jack Kramer observed. "No, Pancho is the master tactician. If you sit next to Segoo watching a quality match, he's analyzing for you why one guy's winning and the other guy's losing in a brilliant running commentary. He's uncanny that way."

That's why his gambling friends liked to be near Pancho during the big tournaments. According to Mike Franks, he could pick winners. "When you get to the quarterfinals he'll pick the one of the eight to win it and get odds. He wins. He's going to be right much more than he's wrong because he knows how they play." As recently as 2005, Pancho was still picking winners. The young American James Blake had climbed back from immense personal and physical setbacks to get into the 2005 U.S. Open, and Pancho, after observing him carefully, said Blake would go all the way to the finals. Nobody believed him, but he was right.

When Butch Buchholz came on to the tour in 1961, Pancho was coming to the end of his greatest playing days, but he beat the younger American constantly and thoroughly. "I learned as much from Pancho Segura as anybody," Buchholz said later. "He taught me to understand my opponent's limitations, check his grip, check and see how his feet are set up. Then your mental computer starts to tell you what the guy can do and can't do. That's pure Pancho. Nobody had a better tennis mind. I tell you, as an amateur going to the pros, I did not understand tennis, but now I think I have a good understanding of the sport because of Pancho." (It is not surprising that Billie Jean King called Pancho the "Ph.D. of tennis.")

All-American Stan Smith, a number-one-ranked player who won both the U.S. Open and Wimbledon singles titles as well as many doubles titles, said of his former coach, "Pancho was able to break down other players' games by watching them for five or ten minutes. He knew how to execute a shot that would be the most effective weapon against an opponent. He taught me how to take advantage of situations and how to put pressure on my opponents. I think of him as maybe the best tactician that I've ever met."

Rod Laver, one of the young Australian virtuosos who also came on to the tour at the time Pancho was quitting, and who is considered one of the greatest tennis players of all time, used to watch matches with Pancho and was amazed at his knowledge of the game. "He was always saying, 'He should have lobbed, he should have come in.' It rubs off on your own game," Laver said.

In spite of the fact that Pancho, by now turned forty, was basically past his best, the two men had several memorable matches together. Laver (known as "The Rocket") appreciated how Pancho had that special knack of summing up an opponent. "When he played Rosewall, he could analyze Kenny's game and use his double-handed forehand with such accuracy it was a shame more people didn't see it. When I was in a match, I always used to remind myself how Pancho did it."

While the Inca Warrior couldn't blow the Rocket off the court physically, he would do it by other means. "I always looked forward to my games with him," Laver recalled. "You felt like you could win, but his knowledge was so great you'd soon start doubting yourself. He had a lot of years on me, but he knew what you were going to do before you did it. He'd change the pace of the ball. He'd fake a drop shot—and it's over your head! His timing was where his power came from. He really ran too—those happy little feet all over the court.

"He'd bring you down to his level. 'I can do that too, Pancho,' you'd say to yourself. 'But you can't do it as well as I can, buddy,' he would shoot back. He'd never let you off the hook. His wheels were turning all the time. You're always asking, 'What's he up to now?'"

In his book *Mental Tennis* Vic Braden wrote, "Segura was one of the best thinkers and strategists I've ever seen in the game and one of the most underrated players in the history of tennis." Braden gives an example of Segura's phenomenal mind game. One day Vic went on to the court and saw Segura all alone, bouncing the ball on his backhand side, hitting down-the-line shots, and then running diagonally across the court as fast as he could. "I watched him for a while repeating that same drill, bouncing the ball and running, bouncing the ball and running, and finally I said, 'Sneaky—you okay? I mean, man, you look like you're on the sauce.'"

Segura turned to Braden and explained that the following day he was playing Pancho Gonzales in the final of a tournament at the Los Angeles Tennis Club. He knew that Gonzales had a continental hammerlock grip. "So when I hit down the line and he has to stretch for his forehand volley, he can only go crosscourt with it, because of the way he holds the racket." As Braden went on to explain, Segura was practicing what he expected to happen next day in the finals. He figured that if he could run and get Gonzales's return of serve, Gonzales would still be over by the alley, the whole court would be open, and Segura could score an easy point. As it turned out, largely by the use of this intelligence, Segura beat Gonzales and won the ten-thousand-dollar-tournament. "This is a wonderful example," Braden said, "of a player who extracted a single piece of data from a broader field of knowledge and used it to evolve a marvelous game plan."

For most of his playing life, Pancho Segura had been dissecting his own and everyone else's game with a shrewdness and perceptiveness that went far beyond most tennis professionals. Now was his chance to put his accumulated data to brilliant effect. Segura turned out to be a born tennis instructor. Not only could he analyze the game better than almost anyone else but, more importantly, he could vividly convey his message to anyone who would listen.

This was the man who showed up one day at the Beverly Hills Tennis Club to be the club's new coach.

On January 25, 1963, the Beverly Hills Tennis Club sent out an invitation to its members. "The nominal reason for this gig is to bid a tearful farewell to Carl Earn [the departing tennis pro], and to meet and welcome his successor, Pancho Segura. Pretty silly: Carl will get better market tips at Hillcrest and everybody already knows Panch. He's even more cheerful and less intelligible than Carl." Further down in the invitation, members were asked to remember, "Free hors d'oeuvres—no greasy kid stuff," and "Shake *both* Pancho's hands."

Carl Earn, who had been on the tour in 1947 with Pancho, helped get him the job. Earn went on to teach at the Hillcrest Country Club. "I left for more money," he said afterward. Later, Pancho was to understand his old friend's move only too well. In 1963, the Beverly Hills Tennis Club did not have much of a tennis program, and the tennis played there was not very serious. It was a place where a select group of 150 mostly Jewish members came together for a game of tennis or backgammon, eat a very good luncheon with good service, and talk movies over a cold drink or in the steam room after the exercise.

The men who got together at the club in those years dominated the Hollywood film industry much as their predecessors, Jesse Lansky, Louis B. Mayer, Jack Warner, Irving Thalberg, and Sam Goldwyn, had dominated it from the beginning of the business. The tennis club was small, with only five courts, and it was hidden behind high hedges on North Maple Avenue, almost impossible to find unless you knew where you were going. Its quiet, exclusive atmosphere offered a striking contrast to the constant swirl of movie-star gossip and celebrity spotlights that fueled the working lives of these Hollywood moguls and their guests.

The makeup of the Beverly Hills Tennis Club was no accident. According to co-founder Larry Bachmann, it was founded in the early fall of 1929 by Bachmann, Milton Holmes, a movie actor under contract to Cecil B. de Mille, and Fred B. Alexander, a top amateur tennis player in the league of Tilden and Johnston. (He was also socially prominent: Alexander Hall at Princeton University was named after his family, who donated it.)

"There was a pertinent reason for starting the club," Bachmann wrote in a history of the club. "At that time the only tennis club was the Los Angeles Tennis Club, which had a rule that excluded those in the film industry and Jews."

At the beginning of the twentieth century, several clubs in the major cities of America were founded as Jewish alternatives to the traditional white-only, Anglo-style clubs owned by the WASP ascendancy. In New York, the Harmonie Club struck back at the exclusive membership rules of the Metropolitan and the Union League. In Los Angeles, the Beverly Hills Tennis Club, as Bachmann explained, was born in response to the restrictions of the Los Angeles Tennis Club.

The Los Angeles Tennis Club was second only to Forest Hills in New York as the top tennis center in the United States, every year putting on the largest amateur tournament in the country, the Pacific Southwest Tennis Championships. As well as nurturing many of the early great players such as Ellwood Vines, Bill Tilden, Jack Kramer, and Richard Gonzales, the Los Angeles Tennis Club was also a fun place for movie stars, attracting tennis players who loved the game like William Powell, Errol Flynn, Clark Gable, and Carole Lombard. Blackballed from these illustrious grounds were some of the biggest names in Hollywood. In response, they founded their own tennis club in Beverly Hills, conveniently close to where most of them lived.

Initially, the club struggled, until Fred Perry, the English tennis champion who had moved to Beverly Hills, and Ellsworth Vines, the top American player of his day, agreed to buy it and put it on more secure financial grounds. With these names as draws, the club quickly began to attract members from the Hollywood community. Barbara Hutton, Cornelius Vanderbilt, Mrs. Irving Berlin, and Dick and Dorothy Rodgers were some of the early supporters.

At the dedication of the new clubhouse in 1931, Fred Perry, Charlie Chaplin, Groucho Marx, and Ellsworth Vines were invited to play a celebration match. It was to be the Americans (Marx and Vines) versus the British (Chaplin and Perry). According to a report that was written up and is now hanging on a wall inside the clubhouse, Groucho Marx arrived to play with twelve rackets and a large suitcase. "When the British were in the lead, Groucho sat down on the court, opened the suitcase and began to eat lunch. He offered tea to Chaplin, leaving Perry and Vines to finish the match."

After World War II, the club became even more successful. Movie stars were always to be found there, however good or bad their tennis. Pauline Betz, the women's champion in the 1940s, used to play there against Robert Taylor—and beat him. There are photographs of Groucho Marx, Barbara Stanwyck, Walter Matthau, and Doris Day at the club in 1957, before Pancho's arrival, along with other celebrities. In 1966 Pancho was photographed with Charlton Heston and the club's president, Harold Willens. The bandy-legged *cholo* had already made an indelible mark on the place.

From the start, it was a completely different life. After scraping a living by performing in out-of-the-way places for a dubious gate, playing night after night as a "semi-servant," as Pancho called it, he was suddenly thrown into a position of authority and power. And his clients were no ordinary tennis novices looking for a little adjustment to their backhands. Pancho found himself surrounded by movie stars, directors, writers, interesting people, crazy people, glamorous people, whose names read like a celebrity encyclopedia from the sixties: Dinah Shore, Doris Day, Julie Andrews, Richard Conte, Shelley Winters, Charlton Heston, Barbra Streisand, Dina Merrill, Kirk Douglas, Robert Evans, Lauren Bacall, Burt Bacharach, Gene Hackman, Carl Reiner, Barbara Marx (later Sinatra), Ava Gardner.

Imagine teaching them tennis. "I'd teach them the grip, the strokes, the fundamentals, try to motivate them to play tennis. Most of them did it for the exercise, rather than for the love of the game. They did it to take a break. Later, I coached their kids."

The club was private and secretive behind its high hedges, but once within the grounds, it had all the amenities members could desire. There was a large patio with chairs and umbrellas overlooking the "center" court, where big matches and exhibition games were played. There was a swimming pool, plus changing rooms and lockers. There was also a steam room and a small shop, which Pancho ran with an assistant.

At the beginning, he and his new family lived in Reeve Drive, about two blocks from the Beverly Wilshire Hotel. He would leave the apartment at around eight o'clock and walk to the club. Later the Seguras moved to Woodland Hills, where their neighbors were Frank Sinatra and the producer Hal Roach. It was a good neighborhood, but it was much farther from the club, and Pancho would have to get up at six or six-thirty in the morning to get to his lessons.

He was assigned court three, a little apart from the others, so that there would be fewer distractions for his students. He would teach three or four hours a day, mostly half-hour lessons, to the movie people and their children. His fee was usually fifteen dollars per hour, twenty-five dollars at the most. Most of his pupils were members, but sometimes, when allowed, he would bring in non-members. His goal was to teach as many hours as possible, since he was paid only for his lessons, plus the money he made from the shop from the sale of tennis balls and other small items.

To make more money, he would try to find time to teach in other places, such as at the tennis academy in Pasadena, where he could earn one hundred dollars in four hours. There, every Saturday morning, he taught the young Stan Smith, a student at the University of Southern California. "We'd play with him for twenty minutes," Smith recalled, "then we'd train from 8:00 a.m. to 12:00 noon, and he would play against us and point out where our shots were wrongly chosen and so on. He played so well and he controlled the point so well that we would really learn a lot." Stan Smith certainly learned a lot. In 1968, he won the U.S. Intercollegiate singles, and the doubles with Bob Lutz in both 1967 and 1968, before going on to a championship career, winning the singles at Wimbledon in 1972 and one singles and four doubles titles at the U.S. Open.

Pancho also worked outside the club by giving private lessons, for instance at the homes of Dean Martin, Kirk Douglas, or Charlton Heston. They would take lessons from him, and they also allowed him to use their courts to give lessons to other people who wanted to be coached by Pancho and who were not members of the club.

From the very beginning, Pancho created something magical at the Beverly Hills Tennis Club. His endearing personality, quick wit, racy jokes, and sexy charm acted like a magnet both to the serious and the dilettante players who came to him for lessons. But more than that, he encouraged an informal atmosphere, where the rich and famous could sit around after their games and feel relaxed. He allowed them privacy, didn't fuss over them, and gave them light-hearted and entertaining tennis instruction as an outlet for their stressful lives.

He was available for all of the members all of the time, making them laugh, amusing them with his witty repartee, inspiring them to want to come back for more. They also grew to respect the little Ecuadorian Indian with his winning ways. On one occasion, Ava Gardner and George C. Scott arrived for a lesson. An aspiring young actor with attitude came up to them and started haranguing the two movie stars about his problems with his agent, and what should he do? "You can start by picking up Pancho's balls so we can go and play tennis," Ava Gardner told him.

Pancho goaded his students, teased them, made them enjoy every moment with him, and always, always encouraged them. UCLA tennis star Stan Canter, who later became a tennis pro and movie producer, played regularly at the club with Pancho. "He got me into the game," Stan Canter recalled. "We played all the time, and I came close to beating him. But I never did." Pancho would give up games as a handicap in favor of his eager opponent, and finally, the young player's luck changed. One day Stan beat him. "The next day I went to my locker and there inside was a whole new tennis outfit. With it was a note: 'For the champ, Pancho.'"

Jeanne Martin, wife of Dean Martin, arrived at the club in 1966. She was very young and very blonde, and she asked Pancho if he thought he could give her tennis lessons. Pancho took a look at her and said, "Do I think I could give you tennis lessons? Oh, baby!"

They became fast friends. "I adored him," she said. "He was a wonderful flirt. And he was the greatest tennis teacher in the world. I would have done anything for him. There are people I've met in my life who have affected me in an intense, almost cosmic way. That's how it was with Pancho."

Through Jeanne Martin, Pancho met other movie stars like Dinah Shore and Janet Leigh. Mrs. Martin would invite Pancho to her house where they all played tennis together. They sometimes had matches on the Martins' private court. Pancho began giving tennis lessons to the Martins' son, Dino. Dino became a close friend of Spencer's. That's how things were at the Beverly Hills Tennis Club in those years of the sixties. It was like a big, extended family, an oasis, where everyone was connected. "During those days the club was a special place," said Joan Emery, daughter of longtime member Arthur Glick, "and its spark and energy had a lot to do with Pancho's presence."

Joan was a teenager then, and she and her friends would come over whenever they could after school and hang out at the club. "We all grew up together there," Joan recalled, "Dino Martin, the Kreiss brothers . . . Spencer, of course. Having Pancho there gave us a place to go, a home, at the club."

"Spencer, of course." For Pancho's dark and handsome son, the club was not only a place to learn to play tennis, but it was where he found a sense of family. "It was my escape," he said. It was also the place where he was able, for the first time, to spend days, weeks, even months, with the Pied Piper of this privileged community—his father.

Pancho with his old friend Bobby Riggs, mid-1950s.
Photo courtesy of the Beverly Hills Tennis Club.

Before a doubles match at the Slazenger Pro Championships at Eastbourne in 1958. *Left to right*: Australians Ken Rosewall and Lew Hoad vs. the U.S. pair Tony Trabert and Pancho Segura. Photo by Arthur Cole/Le Roye Productions

(top) Trabert and Segura battle the Australian champions in a pro tour matchup that plays to sold-out stadiums all over Europe. Photo by Arthur Cole/Le Roye Productions.

(bottom) Segura and Trabert receive the trophy after defeating Hoad and Rosewall 6–2, 1–6, 6–3, 6–4, at Eastbourne in 1958. Photo by Arthur Cole/Le Roye Productions.

Segura, having beaten
Sedgman in five hard-fought
sets in the semifinals of
the London Pro Indoor
Championships at Wembley
in 1960, finally succumbs to
Rosewall in the final, 5–7, 8–6,
6–1, 6–3. Photo by Arthur
Cole/Le Roye Productions.

In spite of their long rivalry,
Segura and Rosewall remain
good friends on and off the
court. Photo by Arthur Cole/
Le Roye Productions.

In later years, Segura (Little Pancho) and Gonzales (Big Pancho) continue to see each other and play together, although both were long retired from the world of professional touring. Photo courtesy of Segura family collection.

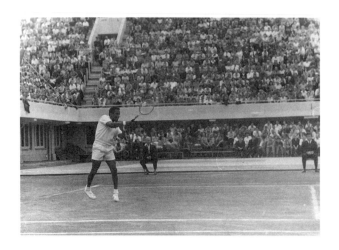

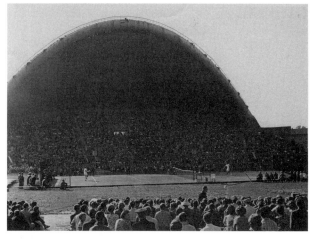

Conditions on the tour ranged from nightmarish (wooden planks over a school basketball court) to this glamorous outdoor stadium in Adelaide, Australia. Photos courtesy of Segura family collection.

Wimbledon 1968—open at last to both professionals and amateurs—allows Segura and Alex Olmedo to enter the doubles championship. Photo by Arthur Cole/Le Roye Productions.

Segura, aged forty-seven, playing his first Wimbledon in 1968, draws a second-round doubles match with Alex Olmedo against the South Africans Gordon Forbes and Abe Segal, in a duel that breaks the record for the longest set ever played at Wimbledon, ending at 32–30. Segura and Olmedo go on to win the match. Photos by Arthur Cole/Le Roye Productions.

Unbelievable! Pancho smiles his irresistible smile after the record-breaking set at Wimbledon in 1968. Photo by Michael Cole.

In his role as coach at the Beverly Hills Tennis Club, Pancho enjoys new friends—actor George Peppard and the sixteen-year-old Jimmy Connors. Photo courtesy of Segura family collection.

In 1968, Pancho begins a relationship with Jimmy Connors that
will take the Ecuadorian master's young student to the pinnacle
of the tennis world. Photo courtesy of Segura family collection.

Pancho teaches Jimmy everything he knows. Jimmy absorbs
every lesson, in the process transforming his game into that of
a world champion. Photo courtesy of Segura family collection.

From left: Jimmy Connors, Pancho, Jimmy's then-girlfriend, Chris Evert, and Pancho's son, Spencer, at the Beverly Hills Tennis Club. Photo courtesy of Segura family collection.

Pancho imparts his wisdom to many other up-and-coming
players, including Stan Smith. Photo by Melchior Di Giacomo.

Pancho becomes coach to Charlton Heston (center) among many stars at the Beverly Hills Tennis Club. Photo courtesy of Segura family collection.

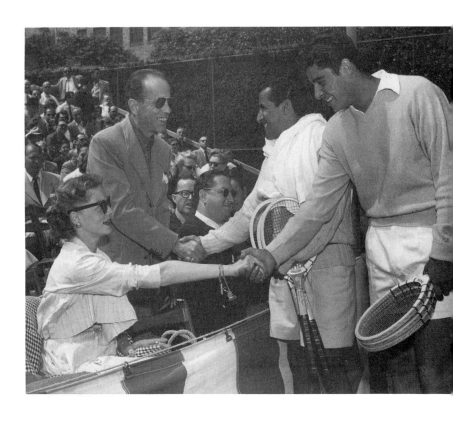

The two Panchos (Segura and Gonzales) receive the admiration of Hollywood legends Humphrey Bogart and Lauren Bacall. Photo by Robert Harland Perkins.

Lauren Bacall shares a joke with Segura and Gonzales at the
Beverly Hills Tennis Club. Photo by D. D. and E. Peter Schroeder.

Dean Martin, one of Pancho's closest friends during his
Beverly Hills years. Photo courtesy of Segura family collection.

Pancho coaches many of Hollywood's great stars, including
Barbra Streisand. Photo courtesy of Boulevard Photo.

Segura is just as popular off the court as on, here with Shirley Temple in Beverly Hills. Photo by Max Peter Haas/European Picture Service.

Pancho's second marriage, to Beverley Moylan Young, takes place in 1961 at the Ecuadorian embassy in London, with the blessing of the ambassador. Photo by Arthur Cole/Le Roye Productions.

Pancho and Beverley at a celebrity event with Richard Burton
and Susan Hunt. Photo by Thelner Hoover.

Pancho with his good friend, the explosively
talented Ilie Nastase. Photo by Art Seitz.

Pancho with Princess Grace of Monaco at a celebrity tennis tournament in Monte Carlo. Photo courtesy of Segura family collection.

Members of the Beverly Hills Tennis Club, Charlton Heston, Dinah Shore, and Jeanne Martin, celebrate their longtime resident pro in an all-day Tribute to Pancho Segura in 1966. Photo courtesy of the Beverly Hills Tennis Club.

(*left*) Pancho with his oldest and most faithful fan, his mother, on one of his visits back home to Guayaquil in the 1990s. Photo by Escobar Jr., Ecuador.

(*below*) In 2002, at the age of eighty-four, Pancho returns to the Guayaquil Tennis Club where he started his ride into the history books, surrounded by the ball boys who still work the courts as the champion once did, hoping for similar glory. Photo courtesy of Segura family collection.

Chapter Ten

Happy Days in Beverly Hills

One of Pancho's more poignant memories during his first year at the Beverly Hills Tennis Club had a historical flavor to it. "I was playing with Charlton Heston when he got a phone call. He walked off the court and came back and told me that Kennedy had been shot."

That was one of the down moments of a decade that seemed never to want to grow up—the sixties. The timing of Pancho's arrival at the Beverly Hills Tennis Club seemed to have been designed by fate. The country's mood by then was in full flight from the sedate fifties—it was wild, fun, energetic, dance all night, party all day, get high on flower power, trip out on free love. Los Angeles was exploding with the acid rock, pop music, and street happenings that were later to help define the sixties. If later it was called the "youth decade," the Beverly Hills Tennis Club was an accurate mirror of the times, for in those early carefree years before the Vietnam War began to take its toll, it was, for many of Hollywood's young people, the perfect place to hang out, play a little tennis, relax, and feel good.

Pancho, as usual acutely sensitive to the spirit of the times, was more than a fun-loving, dynamic, and skilled coaching professional. Perhaps his greatest contribution during those years was that he turned the club into a meeting place for Hollywood's younger generation, the children of film actors, directors, and producers, often abandoned by parents who were busy shooting on location or going to glamorous parties up in the hills.

Joan Emery was a young girl when she first started taking lessons at the club from Pancho. "Of all the teachers I have had, Pancho was the most encouraging," she remembered. "I felt I could do anything with him. He was easygoing and yet he really made me work. He'd play with me and make comments. He inspired me to be good. I'd double fault or net a ball. My first inclination would be to lose my temper, but he would say, 'Great shot, baby!' He made me learn to be a good sport, and at the same time to want to win, and he did it in such a way that *he made me dig into the depths of my soul to play better tennis.*"

Most of the younger set got half-hour lessons. "Half an hour was all you could take," Ronald A. Recht recalled. "He really worked you hard, put you through a very intense drilling, and that was fine. The idea was to do a half hour, and then we would continue to practice and put our lessons to use. He'd come and watch. He was always coaching."

Desi Arnaz Jr. started taking lessons from Pancho when he was about fifteen years old. "In my mind he was the best teacher in the world," he said later. "He taught technique that others weren't even thinking about—drop shots, lobs, spins, the types of shots you needed with a wood racket." But for young Desi, that was not his secret. "His secret was that he enjoyed the game so much himself. He made jokes, laughed, made it fun. He called me, 'My boy.' 'That's it, my boy! Go for it, Desi, my boy!' He was always smiling. Even when you played him, he'd always be smiling. 'Why are you smiling?' you'd ask yourself. It drove us crazy!"

Pancho loved the young people who clamored for his attention. He loved the girls particularly, of course. Joan remembered him telling her, after she had muffed a shot, "It doesn't matter if you don't play great tennis, kid. You're so good-looking you can get the guys anyway." After a lesson, he'd say to his young female students, "Go and play together," hoping they would continue to practice. But then he would laugh and shake his head, saying, "I know you only want to go off with the boys!"

But he also made the kids work hard, demanding fitness, demanding that they exercise, demanding that they always be on their toes. "Get low, baby!" He would cry in his Spanish-accented English, an accent which he never lost. "Get low! Yes, kid, you can do it!" urging them to greater and greater effort. "Every time we had an interaction, he would tell us which way we should have gone, and how to plot strategy," said Ron Recht. Tom Kreiss, another talented young player, agreed. "He got us in shape. Pancho could run you like nobody else. He had a drop shot that you absolutely couldn't read, and you'd always be about to pass out trying to return it."

Tom Kreiss, like all Pancho's pupils, recognized Pancho's greatest gift as a coach. "Once you get to a certain level, it's strategy that makes the difference. That's where Pancho was so brilliant. I'll never meet anyone again with such knowledge of the game."

But it wasn't all work. After the tennis, the kids would hang out and relax. There was a famous chef called Johnny. "He made us unbelievable fried rice." Ron Recht said. "We all ate fried rice every day." There was always the same waiter, who would give them the same food, doughnuts in the afternoon after swimming, and a milkshake before going back on the court. Then there was ping pong. "We were good at ping pong obviously, because we played such a lot of tennis, so we had big ping pong events."

Growing up in Beverly Hills in the summertime, the kids went to the club every day. "I was there along with fifteen, eighteen other kids," Ron Recht recalled, "and we'd all meet there and we'd virtually be there all day. Our parents would drop us off at nine and pick us up at five. We played tennis all day long, and played Marco Polo in the pool, and we all ate together, and we played a card game called Sergeant Major, and then we went back on the court and played, and sometimes they would even let us play till seven o'clock at night."

It was an idyllic time, and Pancho was like a benign guardian, looking after them all. The kids felt close to him because he was Spencer's dad and because he was their coach and because he treated them like grownups. "He was around all the time and he liked talking with us." He was natural with them, and while everyone else was saying "Mr. This" and "Miss That," Pancho insisted on complete informality. "Okay, kid, stay loose!" he would call after them. They loved the way he talked to them—it was always fun and exciting. "Stay loose!"

The boys would take a steam with him, and in the steam room he would regale his young male listeners with stories that their fathers could never in a million years have told their sons. "We would all sit around naked, with our raging hormones, and he would tell us things about sex, outrageous things," Ron Recht remembered, chuckling, "things I remembered all my life!" Pancho let them in on all the secrets of the bedroom that he had acquired, describing problems and pleasures with no holds barred and no embarrassment, in front of his rapt audience. This wasn't tennis, this was real life—with a Latin flavor—and the boys loved it.

He was hardly less outspoken with the girls. Kay Pick, one of the many young women who spent happy hours at the club, said that Pancho had the charm to get away with saying things to women that if other men said them, they would get hit over the head with a baseball bat. But Pancho's wisdom came not only from the locker room. Kay Pick remembered her sister, Kathy, one day remarking about a married couple they knew, "He's so nice and she's such a terrible bitch." Pancho overheard this and quickly responded, "Yes, but you must remember they are married, so something's the matter with the nice one too." Kay never forgot this shrewd insight.

The girls loved Pancho for his wit, his sexiness, his warmth, and his encouragement of their talent. While the boys were trying to rub up against the nubile young Lolitas in the pool playing Marco Polo, Pancho coached his female students to keep fit, work hard, and learn to be in charge of their own lives. He had learned these lessons the hard way, and he was not going to let them hide behind their wealth and privilege for a minute.

He was particularly hard on his own son. Many of Spencer's friends noticed it. Pancho would read Spencer the riot act, not only if he played poor tennis but if he did not do his homework. For Pancho, the specter of his past was never far away. To get a good education and be able to earn money were the prime goals he wanted for his son, to make up for the painful struggles of his own background back in Guayaquil. If he was harder on Spencer than on the other boys, it was because he was determined that his son never experience the curse of poverty. He was determined that Spencer would be financially successful in life—more successful than his father.

At first, it was difficult for Spencer. "They'd all been playing tennis since they were six," he remembered. Compared to them, Spencer had hardly played at all. "There was never anybody to play with," he explained. "We were always waiting for Dad to come home." Arriving at the club as Pancho's son, of course he was a target. "They wanted to get me on the court and beat me." So Spencer was thrown to the wolves on his very first outing. "Of course at first I was way behind, but I soon got to play as well as they did."

Spencer, at twelve years old, was already a gifted athlete. His tennis quickly improved. But it wasn't the tennis that Spencer loved most about the club. It was being with his father. Finally his father was settled, in one place, and not about to leave any time soon. "I was happy being out of the house and with my dad."

Spencer's father was at the center of the action. That's how the boy saw it when he started going to the Beverly Hills Tennis Club. His stepfather had taken him out of his Catholic school ("too much time teaching religion"), and placed him in the public school, next to UCLA, the same school many of the rich kids attended. Some of those kids, in their free time, went to the Beverly Hills Tennis Club and played tennis.

After school, Spencer would go straight to the club and hang out with his new friends and play tennis. Sometimes Pancho would take him home, but often he would go to other people's houses instead. In 1963, shortly after the Seguras arrived, Beverley had a daughter, Maria. "They were wonderful to me at the club," Beverley said. "They all treated the baby as if it were their baby." Beverley loved those years. "It was such fun," she exclaimed. "And so scandalous! Everyone was talking about who was going off with whose wife." They called it "nesting." "We'd say, 'Is he nesting with her?'" Pancho said with a wicked grin.

The new addition to the family made Spencer feel like an outsider once more at his stepmother's house. The three Kreiss brothers, Bobby, Mike, and Tommy, were some of the most important of his friends at that time, and they created a second home for him. While Pancho played tennis and then socialized with the movie people, and Beverley looked after the new baby, Norman Kreiss would scoop up his three sons and Spencer and take them to their house, where he would be fed and allowed to sleep over. Later, as Spencer's friendship with Dino Martin intensified, the Martin family also welcomed him into their home, so during this time if you wanted to find Spencer, he would be either with the Kreisses or the Martins.

With his son taken care of, Pancho continued to galvanize the club, both on and off the court. By his enthusiasm for tennis, he communicated that enthusiasm to the members. By bringing in outstanding professional players to play at the club, and by inviting nonmembers to take lessons from him, he strengthened the club's standing, and made it more democratic.

Thanks to Pancho, all the most famous names in tennis at that time came through the club—Frank Sedgman, Rod Laver, Lew Hoad, Ken Rosewall, Butch Buchholz, Alex Olmedo. Many of them would be playing tennis at the Los Angeles Tennis Club, or in some exhibition or tournament, and would come by to play for Pancho. "We made it a tennis center," Segura declared. Even Jack Kramer would show up.

"It was not unusual for us to be at the club and see Lew Hoad or Rod Laver playing on center court, which, for me as a young boy, was the ultimate," Ron Recht recalled, still with awe in his voice. Pancho would make sure that his young friends got tickets to the Pan-Pacific Tournament at the Los Angeles Tennis Club, and he arranged for them to meet the legendary players. "'Ron, I want you to meet Rod,' he would say. We met all these guys. It was phenomenal. It was every kid's dream."

At the age of thirteen, Tom Kreiss was playing the top players in the world right there at the club, because of Pancho. Tom played in the U.S. Open at the age of thirteen, thanks in part to Pancho. Who else could have made it possible for this young teenager to test his skills against the legendary champions of the game?

Perhaps the most exciting visitor for these tennis-hungry kids was Pancho's old friend and sparring partner, Richard Gonzales. "He practically lived there," Segura said. At this time, Big Pancho was still playing professional tennis and racking up some brilliant victories. He didn't retire until 1970, when he became resident head of the tennis program at Caesar's Palace in Las Vegas. "By that time he was iconic in the tennis world," said Cliff Perlman, who then owned and operated Caesar's Palace. "I liked him a lot, although he was a loner." Gonzales invited Segura to join him in Las Vegas, but Little Pancho wisely refused. "I knew he would be difficult to work for, and I might not last."

The kids at the Beverly Hills Tennis Club were in awe of Gonzales, both for his mastery of the game and for his famous temper. Ron Recht remembered watching him play in the Pan-Pacific Tournament when the moody Mexican-American lost an important game. "He walked to the sidelines quite quietly, then suddenly picked up his racket and smashed it to smithereens on the net post. It was terrifying. He then calmly sat down, picked up another racket, and toweled off."

The two Panchos remained friends. They continued to talk to each other, although often thousands of miles apart. At one point they discussed opening a tennis school for kids together. In 1959, Richard Alonzo Gonzales published his autobiography, *Man with a Racket*, with an introduction by Francisco Pancho Segura. It was a very affectionate piece of writing. One of Segura's comments about Gonzales went like this: "Pancho's no saint. But then did you ever see a saint with a tennis racket?" At the end of the book, there was a question-and-answer session for Gonzales. This was one of the exchanges:

Q: Why was Pancho Segura one of the last players to wear shorts?

A: The answer is obvious when you study his legs.

Their mutual affection, however, never softened their differences concerning women. On one occasion when Segura was working at the club, the two men went out drinking sangria with Ava Gardner, who by all accounts was one of the most beautiful women in the world. Ava took a shine to Gonzales and after a few drinks, started flirting with him, promising they could "do a little flamenco together." But Gonzales would not respond. "I have to get back to my tennis camp," he muttered. Little Pancho couldn't believe his ears! "Ava was furious," he related later, still incredulous. "'You dumb Mexican,' she yelled, 'I'd like to put your head in the toilet!'"

As well as bringing famous people to the club, Pancho also brought young up-and-coming talent to learn from him and practice. Charles Pasarell used to come from UCLA, where he was a student. Another UCLA student at that time was Arthur Ashe, and Pancho invited him over too. In 1965, Ashe won the NCAA singles and doubles titles. For a black tennis player to do so well was unexpected, to say the least. It must be remembered that this was still the sixties, when black athletes were struggling for equal recognition with whites. Pancho was completely oblivious to any such issues. He had no hesitation in bringing Arthur to the club, playing with him, coaching him, and inviting him to give lessons. With Pancho's typical eye to his financial situation, however, he made a deal with Ashe. The lesson cost fifteen dollars; Arthur kept ten and gave Pancho five. Ashe didn't mind. "I was quite flattered that Dinah Shore and Barbara Marx, who was later to marry Frank Sinatra, would even talk to me at the time," Ashe wrote in his memoir *Off the Court*.

Pancho Gonzales also welcomed Ashe to the club, and when he played with him, he gave the younger player some pointers. "Toss the ball more to the right—into the court," he would tell Arthur.

"Lean into the shot." Arthur appreciated the time and attention given to him by the thirty-seven-year-old legend.

Segura amused Ashe with his attitude to the "third world," an expression only recently introduced into global politics at that time. Ashe said that Little Pancho always called Gonzales, Olmedo, Ashe, and himself "the brown bodies." When Ashe won Wimbledon in 1975, Pancho went up to him and said, "Ah ha, the brown bodies are doing much better, I see."

The regular appearances of these stellar players enhanced the prestige of the club. "Because of Pancho's notoriety he attracted the top players and taught at the highest level," said Dr. David White, a member for fifty years. Travis Kleefeld, another longtime member, added that Pancho's presence gave the club a measure of financial security. Membership skyrocketed. It was unfortunate that these advantages did not ultimately rub off enough on the man who made them possible.

To supplement his meager income, Pancho took the opportunity to take side trips whenever he could. He went to Hawaii with Pat Boone. He played in Monte Carlo. He was in Memphis, in April 1968, when Martin Luther King was shot. Pancho was playing tennis at the home of Memphis mayor Henry Loeb's brother. "Mr. Loeb had a fine house with a swimming pool next to the bedroom, because he was wheelchair-bound and would pull himself right from the bed into the pool."

Pancho noticed these things. As soon as he arrived at the Beverly Hills Tennis Club, he began noticing how the Hollywood people lived. He had never seen such rich people as there were in Beverly Hills. Where he came from, nobody ever dreamed of so much money. After ten years scratching out a living on the pro tour, the contrast was breathtaking. The mansions, the cars, the clothes, the restaurants—he could not believe there was so much luxury. It was something Pancho noticed and absorbed, as with everything else in his life. He had come a long way from his impoverished background, but it was never far from his thoughts.

He frequently went to fancy dinner parties in Beverly Hills, where he was served by butlers and given gourmet food and wine, in extravagant surroundings. One must remember that he was a little bandy-legged Indian, just a tennis pro with a strong Spanish accent employed by the local club—yet he was invited to top-level dinner parties given by important movie people. How many tennis pros get to socialize in such a prominent way off the court? It's almost unheard of. But Pancho was one of a kind. All doors were open to him. Everyone loved him, he was intelligent, he amused them, he had a generous heart, and he told wicked stories. And his wife, Beverley, was beautiful and sophisticated, with a quick sense of humor. They were a splendid pair.

Pancho recalled with particular delight a dinner with Spencer Tracy, Jonathan Winters, and Lee J. Cobb, who lived two houses away from him. "One of the pleasantest moments in my life," he said. He also treasured a dinner party at Ray Stark's house, where he sometimes played tennis. One of the guests at the dinner was the Aga Khan. The Aga Khan, like most people, took an instant liking to Pancho, and when he learned Pancho would be playing in some exhibition matches in France, he invited the Inca Warrior to visit him in Deauville.

Later, when Pancho arrived in France, Bettina, the Aga Khan's then-girlfriend, called him and said that the prince was in Ireland racing horses, but he would be back in time to give Pancho a party. And he was. The party was at the historic casino in Deauville and Pancho said it was one of the nicest affairs he had ever attended, "because it came from the heart."

Meanwhile, outside the exclusive confines of the Beverly Hills Tennis Club, dramatic rumblings were being heard in the world of major-league tennis. After a series of failed efforts to open the game to all comers, it was clear that the continued split seriously damaged both the amateur and the professional game. Although Jack Kramer had been regarded as the enemy by the amateur tournament organizers, since he siphoned off all the best players for his professional tour, he had always pushed for open tennis—for the good of the game. Finally, he saw his wish come true.

On December 13, 1967, the British Lawn Tennis Association voted overwhelmingly in favor of open tennis. Quickly the other countries followed suit. The effect on the pro players was immediate, and they rushed to enter the Grand Slam tournaments from which they had for so long been excluded. In the following year's French Open Championship, Pancho Gonzales, fit and competitive at forty, made it through to the semifinals, before being beaten by Rod Laver. Ken Rosewall won the tournament.

That same year, 1968, Pancho Segura played at Wimbledon. What a groundbreaking moment finally to set foot on those legendary grass courts after having been denied it all the years when he was playing his best tennis. He entered the doubles with Alex Olmedo, the Chief, his fellow "brown body." They reached the second round, where they were to meet the South African pair, Gordon Forbes and Abe Segal. Their combined ages someone calculated, came to nearly two hundred years!

In his memoir *A Handful of Summers*, Gordon Forbes described the match. They began at about 3:00 p.m. on court three. "The court is like lightning and no one can return service. Pancho Segura is at his best in such matches. The crowds adore him."

The endurance test was only just beginning. It turned out to be one of the hottest days of the year, and St. John's Ambulance Brigade had to work nonstop to revive the heat-affected crowds. As Forbes tells the story:

At 9–all in the first set, Pancho sniffs doubtfully at the Robinson's orange juice [provided to the players]. "Drink it, Poppa," says Olmedo. "Eet's good. The Queen she drinks eet."

At 20–all, Segura serves out a long deuce game, then leans against the umpire's stand. "Don't die on us, Segoo," says Abie. "Let's all four of us finish the match!"

Segura looks up with a broad smile, puts a hand to his heart and says: "She don't stop pumping, keed. She still goes strong!"

At 26–all, the umpire runs out of new balls. He calls for

more. "Never mind the balls, professor," says Segura, "eet is better you change the players!"

At 28–all, according to Abe Segal, Segura turns to Olmedo and says, "Hey, buddy, it doesn't look like we'll make eet to the Playboy Club tonight!"

At 31–30, Forbes lost a long service game and the South Africans finally lost the set at 32–30. This was only the first set, and it took two and three-quarter hours. Segura and the Chief went on to win the match, then lost in the next round to Roger Taylor and Cliff Drysdale. The men's doubles that first open year was won by Tony Roche and John Newcombe. The men's singles title was won by Rod Laver. The set that Segura and Olmedo played against Forbes and Segal was the longest set ever played at Wimbledon. Pancho was then forty-seven years old.

Returning to the Beverly Hills Tennis Club after the thrill of playing in a Grand Slam tournament so long closed to him, and making a Wimbledon record for the longest set along the way, Pancho had to adjust to the fact that his future back home did not look so bright. Even though his social life was played out among the elite of the movie business, his work as a tennis coach was losing some of its luster. His students were mostly celebrities and rich people, or their kids, who played tennis for fun, social life, or exercise. They were not interested in becoming great players.

Pancho lived for tennis. He knew he owed his life to tennis. That's why every match he played meant so much to him. "When you come from where I come from, it means everything." It was hard for him to understand people who did not have that commitment. He grew impatient with students who did not care as much as he did for the game. "I like to see people who show desire," he said. "People who fight hard to improve their game." Most of the players he worked with at the club had the desire only to have fun, chase girls, go to clubs, party all night.

Vic Braden understood this. "Pancho was much happier when he was working with someone who was a good player," he observed. "He had little patience with the ones who didn't have much talent."

It was at this moment, after several years of frustrating interaction with people who tended to care more about their Ferraris than their forehands, that a sixteen-year-old kid appeared at the club and gave Pancho the opportunity of a lifetime—a raging, raw talent for Pancho to shape into a champion.

Chapter Eleven Jimbo Rules!

Jimmy Connors was born on September 2, 1952. His mother was Gloria Thompson, only child of Al Thompson, a St. Louis policeman, and his wife Bertha. Gloria's parents were both athletic (Al Thompson was a boxer, suggesting the pugilistic instincts characteristic of the Connors family). Young Gloria grew up playing tennis in East St. Louis, scene of devastating race riots in 1917, and still a rough neighborhood, compared to the more swank part of the city on the other side of the river. Gloria became a very good player, a junior champion and a regular on the national circuit. During those days she met Pancho Segura, Bobby Riggs, Pauline Betz, and some of the other major players, and being very pretty as well as a good player, she was a popular member of the tour.

In the late 1940s she quit the professional game and returned to East St. Louis, where she became a tennis instructor. There she met James Connors, a politically well-connected city employee, whose father had been mayor of the city. Gloria and James Connors got married, had their first son, Johnny, in 1951, and Jimmy a year later. Both boys were introduced to tennis early, by their mother and their grandmother, Bertha (who was known by the boys as "Two-Mom," for her constant presence in the family and maternal interest in her two grandchildren).

Mother and grandmother set the boys to learning tennis their way, which meant less of the serve-and-volley game introduced by Jack Kramer and more of the heavy, consistent baseline game that women then preferred to play. According to Joel Drucker, author of *Jimmy Connors Saved My Life*, Gloria Connors was responding to the "other side of the tracks" mentality that motivated her throughout her life. For instance, the leading instructor in St. Louis was Bill Price, who admired Kramer's big game and taught it to his students. Gloria rejected that, not only for practical reasons (women were at that time still inexperienced at volleying) but because, in Drucker's words, "[Price] was a rival from across the river, and though he was no country club patrician, he existed to be hated—both stylistically and personally."

Whatever the reasons for Gloria's teaching approach, Jimmy Connors grew up learning to hit long, heavy, baseline drives, each one struck with a rock-solid intensity that was instilled in him by his mother and grandmother. In fact, whenever Jimmy tried other techniques, such as half volleys or drop shots, they yelled at him to stop. For these two women guiding him, fueled by competitiveness and a sense of exclusion from the social side of St. Louis, there was no toleration for the appearance of "weakness" in making shots. In Drucker's words, "Tennis wasn't art. It was combat."

The only technical concession his teachers made was to allow him to use a two-handed backhand, which he had from the start found more comfortable. Their decision was a wise one: Jimmy Connors's backhand became one of the most ferocious strokes in the history of tennis.

Throughout his formative years, Jimmy played tennis day in, day out, under the unrelenting scrutiny of Mom and Two-Mom. While his older brother dropped out of the race, Jimmy made it clear he was in it for the long term. In the debilitating humidity of the St. Louis summers, he played. In winter weather, he played. The two women fed him ball after ball, over and over, hour after hour, analyzing his swing, his hip movements, his footwork, his stamina. Jimmy absorbed it all, uncomplaining. After all, for every waking moment of his young life he was getting the undivided attention from the two most important women in his life. What boy could ask for anything more?

When Jimmy was ten, he started playing in the National Boys' tournaments at the Manker Patten Tennis Club in Chattanooga,

Tennessee. He did well over the next four years and was ranked in the top ten juniors, but he did not win many titles. He was not a sensation. He was small and not as strong as some of the other players. His astonishing training had yet to come to fruition on the court.

A revolutionary new addition to the game began to help him change that. The Wilson T-2000—a tennis racket made of aluminum instead of wood—was introduced, and Jimmy immediately took to it, not only for its jazzy looks but because it had a lot of power if hit in the right place. Most players found controlling the ball quite difficult with this erratic new racket, but after so many years of accuracy drills, Jimmy's consistency in hitting ground strokes made the racket an ideal weapon.

In 1968, Jimmy won his first national singles title in the boys' sixteen championship. That year, Gloria Connors came to a major decision about her son's future. With that first national title, she knew he had it in him to be great, but she also sensed that she could not take him any further herself. "I had my game, and I had my strokes and whatever it took," Jimmy said later, "but I needed something more."

When Pancho Segura came through St. Louis that year on a tour, Gloria made arrangements to meet him. "Pancho," she said, "I've got this kid. He's a good player." Pancho laughed. "Yeah, yeah," he said, "I get that from every parent." But Gloria and Pancho had been friends a long time, and had played tennis together, so Pancho listened to her and finally agreed that Jimmy should move to California and be coached by Pancho. "You want to come to Beverly Hills?" Pancho said to Jimmy. "I'll get you in school where my son, Spencer, goes to school."

So Gloria and Bertha scooped up the young tennis player, leaving behind his father and brother in St. Louis, and moved to California.

Jimmy was sixteen years old.

At first the move was a difficult one. Jimmy had family, friends, and a home he had always known, and he was going into a very different environment. "The first day I got off the plane," he recalled, "I spent a day in Beverly Hills, and we were walking to a restaurant and I said to my mother, 'I don't want to do this. I want to go home.' So my mom said, 'Look, why don't you go see where Pancho teaches, and just drive around a little bit.' So I did and I came back that night and I said, 'Listen, I'm not going anywhere. I'm staying right here.' And the next day, my second day in Beverly Hills, I got up and went to the tennis club where Pancho was, and never left."

Gloria's instinct and timing were inspired. Of all the tennis player–coaches in the world at that time, only Pancho could have been such a perfect fit for the young prodigy. "Gloria liked the way I played," Pancho said. "Because I was small, I played with two hands, and because of my ability to run, and my ability to fight for every point, and my concentration. Jimmy liked it too. 'You play like me,' he said."

All that was true, but there was an underlying motivation behind Pancho's game that was more subtle to estimate. "Basically my game was formed by then," Connors said. "My mom had given me the kind of tennis, the strokes and skills that I was to play with through my whole career. But what Pancho really gave to me was everything else. He gave me the mental aspect, because I was taught by women to play in a man's game, and I needed a male influence to change that. Pancho and I were about the same size, both small compared to many of the other players. We understood each other's advantages and disadvantages. But it was the thinking part of the game, the understanding of the game, the knowledge of what it took to win, that he was able to give me. My mother recognized that. I mean, how smart was she to understand that?"

Very smart, indeed. Jimmy Connors had learned his tennis from his mother and grandmother, and they taught him how they played, which was, in his words, "basically an easygoing game. It was compact, and it happened to be just the kind of game that fit my style and my personality. But it was a ladies' game, and what goes into your head and your mind when you go into a match is something else, and that has to be added to the mix."

"He was very conservative," Pancho said later. "He played too safe. I tried to tell him, if you're ahead a point, gamble a little. Be more aggressive. But don't gamble or be aggressive when you're behind. In other words, be protected by the score. You have 30–love, 40–love, you can afford to go for an ace when you're serving. When you're returning, you can afford to go for placement. In other words, take chances when you're ahead—if you call that taking a chance!"

Pancho saw in Jimmy initially a player who was sometimes too tight, too careful.

He liked long rallies and he would never go to the net. I told him when to play defense, when to play offence. I had to teach him how to lob. If he's five feet behind the baseline, I'd ask him to play defense, but throw in a lob, which will give him time to come back to the middle. I taught him how to use his side of the court wisely, how to go for big shots, take into consideration the score, the graphic position, or where he's hitting the ball from, and the weakness and strengths of his opponent. If the guy has a weakness and likes low balls, we're going to give him the high ball. If he doesn't like the net, we're going to play short and low, so he has to come to the net. Have a plan. Have a plan of playing winning tennis.

Jimmy listened, transfixed. And learned. "I was so well prepared for everything," he observed, "my strokes, my footwork, all the groundwork had been laid for this very moment with Pancho. It was a perfect fit."

For Pancho, it was an unimaginable stroke of luck. All the knowledge he had accumulated over his years of struggle and hard work would now be called into play. All his intelligence, cunning, and psychological skills would be used in the best way possible to further the career of a gifted young player. All Pancho's passionate love for the game would now be passed on to this eager pupil, who could hardly wait to follow in the steps of the master.

"Connors was very coachable," Pancho said simply. "He believed in me and what I was doing." The experienced little bandy-legged Ecuadorian, almost from the first practice session, knew what he had on his hands. "I am teaching the next world champion," he told his son, Spencer.

"I was a sponge," Connors said. "I was able to absorb everything he said. I'd take what I wanted, and what didn't fit me, I'd let go. But I wouldn't let it go out the window. I'd let it go into the sidecar, so that if I ever wanted it, I could always go back and say, 'What was that?' But basically I absorbed everything. And once you absorb everything and you're confident in what you have absorbed, then whatever else you have inside you comes out that much easier."

It was an intense time. Jimmy would be on the court three or four times a day, hitting balls, playing, and learning. "If somebody said, 'Hey, Connors, come on over here, let's play,' Pancho would say, 'Go hit some with him.' And I'd say, 'Yes, sir. Right now.' Not because he told me to, although that was part of it—but because I wanted to. And I knew that if he told me to, then it must be right. So when you say it was a perfect fit, it was a perfect fit. And my mom allowed that to happen."

The Beverly Hills Tennis Club was also a perfect fit. "It was an unbelievable scene, all the people who were there," Jimmy recalled. "And that was all Pancho. He'd arrange a game. He'd get us together. There were always kids around for me to hit with, so it was, 'Connors, go play with Pancho Gonzales' or 'Go play with Stan Smith' or 'Go play with Charlie Pasarell.' Not a problem. And at the end of the day I'd sit around, have a Coke or take a steam, and laugh, and have fun, and talk about the day's tennis, and who am I playing tomorrow, and who's coming next week? Can I play anybody? Or if not, can I play you, Pancho, for thirty minutes?"

There was no stress, no strain, no obligations, no anything except trying to become a better tennis player at the age of sixteen years old. "So how perfect a life was that? My mom wanted me to become good at tennis and get an education. And that's what I did."

The other members of the club watched as Pancho transformed Jimmy's game. Pancho would haul out a bucket of balls and feed them, and Jimmy had to hit the bucket. Then hit the corners. Then the bucket again. This exercise went on for hours, without a pause, on and on, Jimmy striking the ball over and over, aiming at the bucket, then the corners. "We knew he was good," long-time member David Blum recalled later. "But he was small, with no big strokes, no power. He became the product of Pancho Segura." Young Tom Kreiss, watching them, thought that Pancho's contribution was his brilliant court analysis: "Once you get to a certain level, it's strategy that makes the difference." Blum suggested that perhaps the most important lesson Pancho imparted to Jimmy was grit. "He never gave up. The line between great and good is very small. It is that determination that separates the two—and Jimmy had it."

Pancho coached to win, but he also had his own quite brilliant way of letting his pupil deal with defeat. His psychological understanding of the player's needs at these times was astonishingly sophisticated for someone who had never opened a psychology textbook. "Jimmy would get down on himself when he lost, but I would not let him," he explained.

I would let him cool off for two or three days, never belittling or demeaning him. I would never, ever get down on him. A good coach should be smart enough not to do that. I'd always pull him up. Later, I might say, in the conditional tense, "You could have done this, you might have done that," but the point is the match was history. If he came to me saying, "Coach, I should have done this, right?" I would say, "Yeah, but we'll talk about it tomorrow. It's history."

Pancho remembered being hard on himself after a loss. "I wasn't a happy loser," he confessed. "I wouldn't want to look at myself in the mirror. 'You stupid Indian, you! That was some big gringo!'"

The two would reconstruct Jimmy's play, from tapes or memory, to see what happened. "We'd talk about it until we decided how to deal with any problems, or how to improve them. If we fail in execution, we must do a drill, reconstruct the play. Jimmy was always ready. You could feel the electricity in his play, his desire."

Coach and pupil spent hours together, on and off the court. Pancho would write things down for him on cocktail napkins, plan strategies, what to do at 30–40 or 15–30. "I would scout his opponents, tell him, 'The guy's a good competitor, he's a front runner.' Front runner in tennis means the guy gets in front of you 3– or 4–love and plays great for a few minutes, then he cools off." Every aspect of the game Pancho had learned he now passed on to his student.

"There comes a point where things are bouncing off your head so much that it becomes natural," Jimmy commented. "Like I said, I was a sponge. The fun part was that the better I became, the more I was able to incorporate Pancho's instructions and then try something of my own. I'd try something that might work, and then I had two things that work. Those times gave me a bit of mystery about myself and the game that made it even better for me."

Jimmy worked hard—day after day after day. "I never let up one minute. But tennis came very naturally to me, as a player and as a competitor. That's what I wanted to do. *There was nothing else in the world that I'd rather do.*"

If that sounds familiar, it's because Pancho Segura felt exactly the same way. "I saw myself in him," Pancho said. "He played with the same outlook, the same concentration, the same trance-like performance on the court. He believed in himself—that was the best thing. This left-handed kid was going to be a great tennis player."

Pancho pushed him mercilessly, made him compete with older, stronger players. "Everybody thought I was crazy, because he was small—his competitors were Roscoe Tanner, Dick Stockton, and Erik van Dillen, all bigger than Jimmy. Even Jack Kramer thought he was too small. He said that Jimmy didn't have the serve. 'Jack,' I said, 'Jimmy has a return of serve that's unbelievable.' And I was right. He beat all of them. I knew that from the very beginning. I told everyone, 'This is the guy who's going to kill them all.'"

Some people criticized the way Pancho pushed his kid, pitting him against the more experienced players at the Los Angeles Tennis Club, for instance. One of Pancho's regular tricks was to bet money on Jimmy's matches. He found that it reinforced his concentration and the will to win. "Jimmy was brash in those days," remembered David White. "But it was backed up with ability. I remember one time I played a doubles match with Connors against the two Panchos. Connors played ferociously, poaching all the time, invading my territory, not allowing me to blow a shot. I never saw a kid who wanted so badly to win. And we did win—we beat Gonzales and Segura!" Dr. White learned afterward that their two opponents had money on the match. "Connors collected money from the two Panchos, that's why he wanted to win!"

What was there for Jimmy apart from tennis? He managed to find time to go to Rexford High School, where Spencer Segura had also transferred. In a short time, he and Pancho's son became close friends. They were almost exactly the same age. Spencer introduced him to the other members of the Beverly Hills Tennis Club, who welcomed Jimmy, this unsophisticated kid from St. Louis, who knew nothing about Hollywood or Beverly Hills or movie people or fast cars. "I'd stand back and observe, really," Jimmy said. Spencer soon taught him otherwise.

They would go to Jack Hansen's house (which formerly belonged to Charlie Chaplin) and party. They would go to the Daisy, the hot nightclub at the time. Spencer had become a good friend to Dean and Jeanne Martin's son, Dean Jr., known as Dino. He took Spencer under his wing, buying him clothes, welcoming him into his parents' huge mansion, introducing Spencer to his fast lifestyle. "Everybody loved Dino," Spencer said. "My dad loved him, too, and coached him and tried to give him advice. But there was really no advice you could give him. He knew perfectly well how to handle himself. He never did things that would take him down. In that sense, he had no boundaries."

Dino Martin was a year older than Spencer and Jimmy, and all three of them had something in common they would never think of discussing. Dean Martin loved his son but was a remote father and was often on the road doing his double act with Jerry Lewis. Lewis noted later in his memoir *Dean & Me* that being the son of Dean Martin was no picnic. Like Spencer's and Jimmy's fathers, Dino's dad was not really present in his life. It is hard to know how damaging that was to a young boy, particular the son of one of the most popular heartthrobs of the age. (In 1987, Dino Martin was killed when his jet fighter crashed into the San Bernardino mountains; a tragic end to a life, that, without boundaries, never found real fulfillment.)

The three gifted, tennis-playing friends spent a lot of time together, both on and off the court. The dark, dashing Spencer; the blond, handsome Dino; and Jimmy, with his Beatles-style haircut, must have made a colorful trio as they roared around the streets of Beverly Hills in Dino's Ferrari, leaving behind a trail of broken hearts.

Desi Arnaz Jr. also spent time with the threesome. ("They were like four gangsters, with girls lined up in the alleys," Pancho commented later in a tone of jealous admiration.) Dino and Desi had had a rock-and-roll band since grammar school, and Desi was already starting to act professionally in his mother's show, *I Love Lucy*. These children of show business grew up fast during those years.

Yet even if Jimmy played around with Spencer and the other kids, he was always home early, under the eagle eye of his mother and grandmother. He stayed away from the sex, drugs, and rock-and-roll that most of the others indulged in, always thinking about tennis and protecting himself. "Jimmy was never a redneck, you know," Spencer said. "He was really a down-to-earth, street-smart kid from the Midwest. I think what really separated him was that he had his mom and Two-Mom with him all the time. Who travels like that, with two moms?"

Some of the other kids sensed Jimmy was different, not only because of his background but because of his obsessive commitment to tennis. "We mostly had family money," Tom Kreiss observed, "or family businesses we were going into, so for us tennis was fun but not the be-all and end-all. Jimmy only had tennis. He was really hungry. Tennis was his whole life."

Tennis was his whole life. How well Pancho understood this kid! With Jimmy's father entirely absent from his son's life, and with Gloria, "Glo" as she was called, always at Jimmy's side, Pancho was not only a teacher but a father, a male mentor Jimmy could look up to and respect. They had disagreements, of course, but never serious ones. Jimmy's main bone of contention with Pancho was that he made him cut his hair too short. "There were times, seriously, when Spencer and I would go and get a haircut and Pancho would send us back. He said, 'Your hair's not short enough. Go get your hair cut properly.' So I would say, 'Yes, Pancho.' And Spencer would say, 'Yes, dad.'"

Pancho also introduced him to all the players who passed through the club. The young tiger was tested, and tested again, by the experienced old pros. When Pancho Gonzales played with Jimmy, Gonzales predicted, "He will be one of the top five players in the world." After two years under Pancho's tutelage, Jimmy was ready for the big boys. By that time, any criticism of Pancho's coaching style had long since been silenced.

In 1970 Jimmy Connors reached the finals of the Southern California Junior Tournament at the Los Angeles Tennis Club, where he beat his clubmate Bob Kreiss in two sets, 6–4, 6–2. This was the first time a reporter noted what were to become some of Jimmy's trademarks—the hunched shoulders, fierce expressions, and cocky swagger of the champion. In August 1970, an article described the explosive talent of the youngster from St. Louis, who, the writer declared, was "a new breed of cat." Jimmy Connors, now aged eighteen, was on his way.

Yet at that time, other junior players were still regarded by the American tennis powers that be as having more potential than Connors, in particular Erik van Dillen, a tall, handsome athlete who seemed to have all the strokes that Jimmy Connors had, with a lot more grace and charm. (Connors's outsider role was, of course, encouraged by his mother, Gloria.) In spite of beating van Dillen, to many observers Connors remained the upstart outsider, while white-shoe van Dillen was the favored one. It's surely possible that Pancho's own tough experiences on the tour with Kramer gave extra depth to his understanding of his cantankerous, "unclubbable" student.

But Jimmy's questionable status would not last for much longer.

In September 1970, he beat the venerable Roy Emerson in three sets in the first round of the Pacific Southwest Open, a statement of intent that did not go unnoticed within the tennis community. It was the most clear announcement yet of the changing of the guard. That same month, Jimmy Connors entered UCLA, along with his friend Spencer. They were both immediately placed on the college tennis team.

The following summer, the NCAA tournament was played in South Bend, Indiana, on the campus of Notre Dame, Jimmy's father's alma mater. Jimmy beat Bobby McKinley in the quarterfinals, in a dazzling match, and went on to win the tournament, the first freshman ever to win the NCAA championship.

Several people noted that Jimmy's father never even showed up at his old school to see his son play. The severance was complete. When James Connors was dying in 1977, Jimmy arrived just in time to briefly hold his hand. But it should also be noted that Gloria had taken Jimmy away on her own when he was still a teenager, basically abandoning her elder son and her husband; these family issues were more complex, however, than the simple assignation of disloyalty or blame.

For Pancho, Jimmy's titles were vindication, if any were needed, that his brilliant pupil was set on the path the coach had mapped out for him. "Jimbo" was readying himself for stardom. They were gratifying moments in an otherwise increasingly difficult time in Pancho's working life.

In 1966, two years before Jimmy Connors's arrival at the Beverly Hills Tennis Club, Harold Willens, the president of the club, created Pancho Segura Day, "to honor our ex-pro's twenty-five years of participation in the game." The committee consisted of Arthur Ashe, Janet Leigh, Sam Match, Charlton Heston, Mrs. Dean Martin, Mrs. Kirk Douglas, Jack Kramer, Dinah Shore, and Richard Zanuck. On the final evening of the Australia–United States Challenge Match, a ceremony honoring Pancho Segura was held in the Pan-Pacific Auditorium in Los Angeles, "to commemorate the twenty-five years of active participation in the World of Tennis for this great, colorful, warm human being." Awards and gifts were presented, "flowing out of the respect and affection in which he is held."

In fact, the event was a disguised way to raise money for Pancho. His close friends knew that he was in financial difficulty and put on this extravaganza to show their support. "People paid to participate," Jeanne Martin explained later. "I got together all the photographs of his tennis-playing life, and we printed a silver celebration program with all the big names on it, and the money raised that night was given to him. It meant so much to me that we could help do that for him."

But the private board meetings of the club told a different story. Not everyone adored Pancho the way the kids and most of the members did. Some players, who had never seen a double-handed forehand before, complained that Pancho's strange, anomalous stroke got in the way of his teaching, since everybody else hit the stroke with one hand. Others may have resented his outstanding success with all the good-looking women at the club and his wicked reputation as a seducer. Perhaps Pancho's increasing preoccupation (and use of court time) with the young outsider, Jimmy Connors, did not help matters.

Pancho's continuing battle to make ends meet at the club was reflected in the minutes of the various board meetings held during his tenure. As early as 1963, Pancho had asked for more funds during the club's slow period, and it was suggested that members pony up twenty-five dollars each to support their pro. Over the following years, Pancho requested that the pro shop be expanded, to sell a more adequate line of tennis clothes, supplies, lingerie, cigars, cigarettes, popcorn, and so on, so he could see more profit from the sales. He asked for an additional food allowance for entertaining guests and celebrity visitors. (His one hundred dollars per month was later upped to four hundred dollars.) When the courts were being resurfaced, he asked for a supplement since he could not teach.

In September 1969, he asked for more courts to be opened up for teaching (his only source of income), but members balked at this, arguing that there were not enough courts for themselves and their children. And perhaps the last straw for the struggling pro, in April 1970, it was proposed that Pancho not be allowed to teach at all on Wednesdays, since the club (now so popular it was oversubscribed), was facing the problem of members who complained they could never get enough court time.

In effect, the club was taking away his livelihood, and the increasing restrictions on his ability to earn money forced Pancho to think of alternative employment. He could not give lessons any more to nonmembers, or if he did, they would not be allowed in the locker room. Some of these men were CEOs of large companies and did not appreciate this treatment. The initiation fee for membership in 1970, when Pancho left, was eight thousand dollars—about sixty-five thousand in today's dollars. "The very people who had made the club so great in the first place were now being excluded," Spencer Segura observed later. "If you shut down the membership, you are left with the accountants." The older members were not interested in tennis as a serious sport, they simply wanted to play doubles and then have a steam and a drink. With little hope for change, Pancho knew his days there were numbered.

Just as he was beginning to get truly restless at the Beverly Hills Tennis Club, a man came to talk to him about starting a tennis program in an entirely new type of athletic club. The man was Merv Adelson, an entrepreneur and real-estate mogul in Las Vegas who was developing a resort in Carlsbad, California, just outside San Diego. It was called La Costa.

In 1970, the year of Jimmy Connors's sensational debut on the national tennis circuit, Pancho was suddenly being offered the chance to leave the place where he had nurtured his young protégé, the place where he had made friends with some of the biggest names in the entertainment industry, and to move to a new environment that would open up all sorts of new opportunities for him. On December 28 of that momentous year, Segura sent a letter to Joseph Zoline, the president of the club, telling him of his offer to be made program director at La Costa and announcing his resignation. His letter tells of the good years he has had at the club, and of his regret at taking this course, and offering to continue his services in which his consultation might be of benefit to the club.

The board of directors reluctantly accepted Pancho's resignation. As an indication of how many of them felt about his departure, an anonymous member made these remarks to the board when they began discussing a replacement:

> Ernest Hemingway used to tell a story about an old Rolls Royce which he owned and operated during his sojourn in Paris: "I sold it," he said, "because every time I parked it any place, somebody would come up, pound his hand on a fender, and say, "They don't make them like this anymore."
>
> And so it is with Pancho Segura. There is no "replacement."

If the older members were regretful, the young ones were devastated. Pancho had expanded many of their lives, imparted to them his worldly wisdom, given them an oasis, a center, and had created warm friendships. His personality had drawn them in like a magnet, and his departure meant not only the loss of their beloved tennis pro but the loss of their partner and comrade. "It was very sad when he left," Tom Kreiss said. "I missed him right from day one," Ron Recht agreed. "Without him, we didn't know what to expect. All of us were sad."

Pancho was now fifty years old and about to enter the third phase of his extraordinary career in tennis, leaving behind a huge hole in the hearts of those who knew him, along with a repertoire of jokes and stories that entertained everybody and were mostly unprintable. As tennis commentator and author Joseph B. Stahl said in a short memoir of Pancho Segura: "Pancho could read a telephone book out loud, and it would sound like he was telling a dirty joke." Segura was now as much an entertainer as the Hollywood comedians he had come to know during his years at the club.

But with Jimmy Connors, his star pupil, having left the nest and gone away to UCLA where he was already breaking all barriers to tennis stardom, Pancho was ready to move on. At La Costa, the "pigeon-toed warrior," as Beverly Hills Tennis Club member and former *Los Angeles Times* executive Charles Schneider called him, was taking a position where at last he could get paid what he deserved, in a glamorous setting, at a time when the tennis world was about to explode.

Chapter Twelve Lows and Highs

Rumors constantly swirled around the origins of La Costa. In an article Joel Drucker wrote for the *San Diego Weekly Reader* in 1995, Pancho told the writer simply that "the boys wanted me to come and build up the tennis. I guess you could say they made me an offer I couldn't refuse. They needed me. When this place started, tennis was a joke."

The use of the word "boys" of course sets up alarm bells in certain quarters. According to several newspaper and magazine investigations, La Costa, in Carlsbad, California, was founded in the early 1960s by characters with links to Las Vegas (real-estate developer Merv Adelson and his partner, Irwin Molasky), the Teamsters Union, and the Mafia. In 1964, the Teamsters (led by Jimmy Hoffa) loaned four million dollars to La Costa, and later the Central States Pension Fund, "a Teamsters offshoot Hoffa formed to benefit his friends in the Mafia," according to the *San Diego Reader*, put more than ninety-seven million dollars into the resort.

Merv Adelson's role has always been in dispute. "There was always that question about Merv: is he or isn't he connected?" former HBO chief executive Michael Fuchs once said. Both the *Wall Street Journal* and *Penthouse Magazine* wrote articles suggesting that Adelson and the Mob were in cahoots. His circle of friends always strenuously denied it, even after Adelson was arrested in 2003 and revealed as bankrupt. "Merv wouldn't know a mobster if he sat next to one," said his partner, Irwin Molasky.

Whatever the truth, Merv Adelson was the ideal person to transform La Costa into a thriving and exclusive resort for the big Hollywood figures of the late 1960s and early 1970s. His first big financial success was in transforming the then-modest city of Las Vegas, building Sunrise Hospital, and promoting other large real-estate developments. In 1969 he returned to Los Angeles and founded Lorimar, which became one of the most successful production companies in the world, with shows such as *The Waltons*, and later *Dallas* and *Dynasty*. Adelson soon became the epitome of a Hollywood tycoon, permanently tanned, with fast cars, huge mansions, beautiful women on his arm, and film and TV celebrities vying for his attention. (He was briefly married to Barbara Walters.) He loved hobnobbing with the big movie and TV moguls, and with the charm and energy of his personality, talked them into leaving their palaces in Beverly Hills and driving down to La Costa, where they were treated like royalty.

Merv Adelson had seen how popular Pancho Segura was with the movie people who came to the Beverly Hills Tennis Club. He had seen Pancho's ease with the big stars and how much they adored him. Adelson realized what an attraction Pancho would be at La Costa, bringing in the people Adelson wanted to give the place the glitter and glamour he was looking for. It was a no-brainer to offer the entertaining, Ecuadorian tennis pro a good financial deal and install him as the tennis program director of what promised to be the biggest and most exciting resort in California.

Shortly after his arrival, Pancho was having dinner with Desi Arnaz Jr. in his house in Del Mar, about fifteen minutes away from La Costa, along with Jimmy Durante, another friend who lived close by. (Desi Sr. had moved there after his divorce from Lucille Ball.) "Desi and I spoke Spanish to each other, of course," Pancho said. "He would invite me to dinner for rice and beans, as we called it—*arroz con pollo*. That night Jimmy said to me, 'You know, Pancho, you're working for the boys.' And I said, 'But I'm the only one who has a contract!'"

Indeed he had a contract, the first proper contract in his working life since leaving the pro tour. At the Beverly Hills Tennis Club there was no contract. At La Costa, he had a yearly contract, a condominium on the La Costa estate, and the rights to the profits from the pro shop, which Beverley ran. (Later he bought his own condo and then sold it for a huge profit.) By the end, Pancho was making at least one hundred thousand dollars a year. "It was heaven in those days," Pancho recalled. "The boys spent lots of money, and it became the place where all the movie people came."

Just as Merv Adelson predicted, the stars flocked to La Costa. Burt Bacharach, Ava Gardner, Burt Reynolds, William Holden, Grace Kelly, Merv Griffin, and Ann-Margret were some of the stars of the 1970s who came to La Costa to enjoy the spa and play golf or take a tennis lesson with Pancho. Sports heroes like Mickey Mantle, businessmen like Kirk Kerkorian, and jet-setters like Christina Onassis came to La Costa. The owners added more courts, a spa, elegant landscaping, beautiful cabanas to please their distinguished guests. Their marketing was innovative and hugely successful. La Costa introduced the idea of a destination resort, which is now copied all over the world. Celebrities like Frank Sinatra and the Rat Pack performed at La Costa. In 1972, after Jimmy Hoffa finally went to jail, the deputy of the Teamsters Union called a news conference at La Costa to announce their support of Richard Nixon for president. Nixon lived at San Clemente, not far from Carlsbad. La Costa by that time was the most talked-about resort in the country—and the tennis director was at the center of it all. His timing, once again, was impeccable.

In addition, by the beginning of the 1970s, something big was happening in the tennis world. After years of little growth, compared to the media interest in baseball and basketball, suddenly everybody wanted to play tennis. When tennis became open in 1968, the whole atmosphere of the sport changed. It became chic, fun, and above all, a great game to watch. Much of the credit for this new excitement must go to Pancho's extraordinary student from East St. Louis, Jimmy Connors.

The early '70s witnessed Jimmy's relentless march to immortality. After a year at UCLA, to nobody's surprise, he turned pro. In his first year as a pro, he won six titles and earned ninety thousand dollars. In 1973, he shared the number one U.S. ranking with Stan Smith, who had worked so hard with Pancho in Pasadena. Jimmy also became engaged to Chris Evert, the pretty sixteen-year-old sensation of the women's game, creating a paparazzi-perfect couple. In 1974, perhaps his most important year as a tennis player, he won the two great Grand Slams, Wimbledon and the U.S. Open, both finals played against the legendary Australian Ken Rosewall.

At Wimbledon, the score was devastating—6–1, 6–1, 6–4. As the *Guardian* newspaper reporter commented, "Someone stop this senseless slaughter." At the U.S. Open, the slaughter was even more shocking—6–1, 6–0, 6–1. In an article in *Sports Illustrated*, thirty years later, reporter Alexander Wolff wrote, "In 1974 Jimmy Connors ignited a tennis boom with his wicked metal racket, his storybook romance, his vulgar antics, and his renegade behavior."

Jimmy's coach was at his side throughout these triumphs. Pancho knew Rosewall's game intimately, and his masterful off-court plan to beat him was a textbook case of strategy. There wasn't one aspect of the cunning Australian's strengths and weaknesses that Pancho didn't analyze, pick apart, and put back together in a way that Jimmy could later destroy on the court. The results were almost a foregone conclusion. In such a situation, Pancho's knowledge, insights, and intelligence were no match for Rosewall, let alone any player, however good. At that moment, Jimmy was invincible.

Pancho was also on hand to protect his boy from outside influences off the court. At the U.S. Open, the night before Jimmy was to play his final, Chris Evert, who had just won her singles title, came to Jimmy's room in Queens, which he was sharing with Pancho, and said to Pancho, "I want to celebrate with Jimmy." "You can't," Pancho said, "Jimmy has to sleep." Chris begged the coach, almost crying, asking to see Jimmy. Pancho was adamant. "He's got to play in the final, and he's hot. Tomorrow, after he beats Rosewall, you can have him on toast." Pancho was the gate-keeper, the doctor, the psychiatrist and, yes, the parent. This last job description may have cost him just a little too much.

For Jimmy, hardly aware of these backstairs scenes, these two finals were stunning victories, but another match a year later, in his mind, topped them. "I think two of my most important matches were when I beat Rosewall at Wimbledon and the U.S. Open," he conceded later, "but maybe those were not as important as when I beat Rod Laver in the challenge match in Las Vegas."

The match was arranged by Bill Riordan, the manager Gloria had signed on to handle Jimmy's financial career. It was a made-for-television match, to be played at Caesar's Palace, with hundreds of thousands of fans watching it live and on television. "The surrounding atmosphere of that match," Jimmy remembered, "the build-up, the excitement, the crowds, the tennis fans, and the Hollywood people and the personalities, everyone wanting a part of that—it really sent tennis to a new level."

The match took place on February 2, 1975, and as Riordan told *World Tennis* magazine four years later, "The suite was like a fight dressing room a half hour before the match. A tape recorder was blaring. Jimmy was bouncing up and down, screaming obscenities at the top of his lungs. Pancho Segura was sitting there like a fight trainer, yelling, 'Keel him, keel him.'"

The match was a classic battle between the old guard and the new—the brilliant Laver, who was at that time the only person to have won two Grand Slams and nineteen titles in thirteen years of professional tennis, and the young Connors, still almost an unknown, fresh out of California, and a surprise victor in the two big tournaments a year earlier. It was also a battle of personalities—the much-admired, experienced, unemotional, canny little Australian against the bully boy, the aggressive, vulgar, strutting American, whom most fans loved to hate.

Riordan compared it to the Christians being thrown to the lions. The whole crowd was for Laver and jeered Connors as he appeared on the court. Although coaches were not allowed on the court in regular tournaments, on this occasion Pancho was seated on the court, like a boxer's trainer stationed in his corner. As with Rosewall, the master and pupil had brilliantly strategized the match. Once again, Pancho's profound knowledge of the game and analysis of Laver's particular strengths and weaknesses were called into play.

We knew Laver could not handle depth on the forehand side. We played deep on him. We'd get him behind the baseline. The next shot could be short. We knew the minute we hit deep into his left side, the next shot had to be inside the service line, so we could be on top of him. But we'd have to react instantly. Jimbo's reflexes were great. He had quick combination of one, two shots.

Pancho loved recalling that match. "That was an exciting day for all of us. I knew that Laver had no chance. He was playing a guy who was hungrier, much quicker, younger, and fresher. Laver didn't have anything better than Jimbo at that time, with all due respect."

When Jimmy Connors talked about it thirty-one years later, he paid tribute to the inspiring presence of his coach in this media circus of a tennis game. "Pancho was part of that, and sitting on the court helping me get through a match like that made the experience totally incredible. I ended up winning that match, which was quite a feat." Jimmy Connors beat Rod Laver in four sets—6–4, 6–2, 3–6, 7–5. "The King was dead. Long live Jimbo," Joel Drucker wrote.

Jimmy was right to think that that famous match "helped tennis," as he put it. The crazy Bobby Riggs versus Billie Jean King "Battle of the Sexes" in the Houston Astrodome in 1973 had started the hoop-la about tennis as a media event, with the accompanying infusions of big-time money. But Jimmy's hugely watched match against Laver, and another one scheduled three months later against John Newcombe, put tennis on the map for good.

Jimmy's matches, with their circuslike frenzy and thrilling athletic displays were the proof that the advertisers, marketers, and media buyers needed to convince them that tennis could bring in as much buzz, excitement, worldwide attention, and fan participation as the other sports that had for so long dominated the press and the airwaves.

Pancho's noticeable presence in Jimmy's shadow during these high-profile events did not go unnoticed by the La Costa owners, who were thrilled by the growing celebrity of their tennis director. Sitting in Jimmy Connors's corner, Pancho had been discovered by the media; his dark face, shock of white hair, and flashing smile were immediately recognized by the cameras, as he leaned forward intently watching his kid play—and win. As CBS tennis commentator Mary Carillo said, "He's the kind of guy that draws the camera like a magnet."

If Pancho had found the Beverly Hills Tennis Club a stimulating and glamorous environment, La Costa was even more so. With Jimmy Connors now a media star, Pancho was almost as talked about as his astonishing student. He put on celebrity tennis tournaments, attracting major players and stars. He played in them himself, both in the United States and Europe. He went to Monte Carlo with Burt Bacharach and played there. He was invited onto Aristotle Onassis's yacht for a party. He also managed to hit Prince Rainier of Monaco with a tennis ball, while Rainier's wife, Grace Kelly, looked on. ("They said they'd chop my head off!") The prince was not the only famous person Pancho assaulted. Once, at a San Francisco charity tennis event, Pancho hit the legendary tenor Luciano Pavarotti with a tennis ball in his very large opera singer's chest. It was a memorable moment. "The ball came back over the net—and I lost the point!" Pancho recalled, laughing in delight.

But in 1975, the year Jimmy beat Laver and Newcombe in such triumphal fashion, a strange thing happened. He was beaten at Wimbledon by Arthur Ashe, Pancho's old friend and colleague. Nobody could believe it. Connors had come into the final without dropping a set. His confidence was seemingly unshakeable. Ashe was highly regarded, but very few people saw in him the killer instinct that would be required to beat Connors. But as the match progressed, the quiet, thoughtful African-American began to rattle the younger player. On the advice of his friends Dennis Ralston and coach Donald Dell, Ashe returned everything with a slow pace that defanged Jimmy's power in the backcourt. With calculated efficiency, Ashe would chip shots, keeping the ball low, lobbing and volleying so reliably that Jimmy was forced into errors. (Perhaps an added distraction for Connors was that the evening before, he and Riordan had announced a ten-million-dollar lawsuit against Dell, Ashe, and other members of the Association of Tennis Professionals for banning Connors from the French Open and thus preventing him from earning a living. Ashe was naturally furious.)

Ashe won the first two sets with surprising ease, 6–1, 6–1. Jimmy was of course ready to battle back and fought hard in the third set, finally winning it 7–5. On a roll, Connors went on to lead 3–0 in the fourth, before Ashe, coolly sticking to his game plan, once again rattled his opponent into making mistakes. Connors then went into a spiral that lost him the next five games, giving Ashe the lead he needed and assuring him of the title. Arthur Ashe, in one astounding performance, had effectively dismantled Jimmy's game.

Jimmy's ascendancy was stopped in its tracks with this defeat. At the U.S. Open that year, he also lost, to Manual Orantes of Spain—in straight sets. What had happened to this seemingly invincible tennis machine? Where had that brashly confident kid, that ruthless dragon slayer, vanished?

Some people didn't really notice it at the time, but later many observers realized that Connors's inspiration, mentor, and coach, Pancho Segura, was nowhere to be seen during those two fateful Grand Slam matches in 1975. Gloria Connors had requested he stay away. As she watched her son humiliated on Centre Court at Wimbledon, there was no one to turn to for help. Pancho Segura was not even within calling distance. He was as far away as possible, in Carlsbad, California, watching the match on TV. Without him, Jimmy Connors had a great fall, and there was nobody to put him together again. "When he lost to Ashe, a match I feel he should never have lost, we all felt terrible," Spencer Segura said later.

Spencer knew something bad had happened between Mrs. Connors and his father. It was not entirely clear what had caused the rift, but most people thought they could make a good guess—plain old jealousy. Pancho was getting too much credit for Jimmy's remarkable success on the tennis court. What about Mom? The media focused on Pancho, on his training, on his presence at Jimmy's side, urging his boy on, willing him with signs and gestures to play his most brilliant tennis. In the minds of many of the tennis fans watching from the stands and on television, Gloria was just another professional mother.

Gloria was not just another professional mother. She had guided her son from his earliest childhood, and she was not about to let the spotlight be turned on anyone else. "Behind every successful athlete there is a strong person who helped them early on," three-time U.S. Open winner Ivan Lendl said in a 2006 *New Yorker* article. "Mostly, it's fathers, but for Martina Navratilova it was her stepfather, for Martina Hingis it was her mother, and so on and so on. There is a time," he went on, "which is a very hard time to pinpoint, I think—when the parent must step back. . . . I think that when Earl Woods stepped back a little bit was when Tiger really took off as a golfer. It's a delicate balance."

Gloria Connors stepped back briefly, when she handed Jimmy over to Pancho Segura in 1968. But she could not stand it for long, and in 1975 she decided she must take her boy back. Jealousy is a destructive force, and it seriously affected Jimmy's life, both on and off the court. Jimmy's engagement to Chris Evert was broken off, largely owing, it was said, to Gloria's resistance, although Chris herself denied it. The gossip columns also noted the complicating factor of Gloria's one-time dating of Chris's father, Jimmy Evert.

Gloria was also not the most experienced businesswoman in coping with the exploding financial opportunities for her tennis-playing son that had already turned football and basketball players into millionaires. After those Grand Slam victories, Jimmy Connors could have made deals that would have made him very rich, like today's players. Gloria's view of a hostile world preying on Jimmy prevented him from entering into promotional and advertising contracts that a more aggressive and competent adviser would have not only encouraged but insisted upon. Pancho, ever the diplomat, allowed that she was "overprotective." Jimmy retained his passionate loyalty to his mother to the day she died, in January 2007, in Belleville, at the age of eighty-two.

Many people in the tennis business knew that there had been a rift between coach and student, a rift that most saw as damaging to Jimmy's progress in the sport. "He was Jimmy's guru," said one-time South African tennis champion and big-league promoter Owen Williams. "Everybody knew he was the brains behind Jimmy. We were all in the stands watching him. Jimmy was a better tennis player than Arthur Ashe by far. But of course people loved Arthur."

Vic Braden agreed with this assessment. "I used to watch Pancho teach Jimmy every day at the Beverly Hills Tennis Club. Pancho was so brilliant, and he knew Jimmy had a certain spirit inside. He was the smartest coach in the world for Jimmy, and I never ever heard a word of thanks." Joel Drucker put it in harsher words: "'Erased from history,' is the concept novelist Milan Kundera used to describe the Soviet regime's treatment of Czech leaders," he wrote in his article for the *San Diego Weekly Reader*. "Connors has similarly purged Segura. Since the '70s he has constantly referred to Gloria as his only coach."

"Inside the game, we all know what Segura did for Jimmy," Peter Bodo, a senior editor at *Tennis Magazine*, said recently. "But

Pancho was around at a time when tennis coaches were less in the spotlight. The casual sports fan was not really aware of them. Today, Brad Gilbert is as famous as a coach as some of his players. Pancho would have been on TV being interviewed day and night about Jimmy if it had been happening now."

Jimmy Connors went on to win many more tournaments, including the U.S. Open in 1976, 1978, 1982, and 1983, and was rated in the world's top ten for sixteen years, a record for longevity only beaten so far by Pete Sampras. Jimmy's abrasive personality, his fist pumping, crotch holding, and other antics on the court finally, after many years of hostility, brought the fans to their feet in admiration. He played tennis like nobody else had ever done, and he transformed the game for future generations. "Some people came out to see me win," he said in Alexander Wolff's *Sports Illustrated* story. "Some came out to see me lose. And some came out to see me have a hard time but not lose, because they wanted to come back the next day and see me again."

Whenever there are rain delays during the Grand Slam tournaments each year (usually during Wimbledon), the fourth-round match between Jimmy Connors and Aaron Krickstein in the 1991 U.S. Open is often played on TV, as an example of Jimbo at his most outrageous, shocking, theatrical, and relentless, performing in a draining duel that Connors finally won—at the age of thirty-nine. Connors later told *New York Times* sportswriter Harvey Araton that that match was the most fun he'd ever had at the Open, or on any tennis stage. Poor Krickstein.

Pancho rarely talked afterward about the estrangement. "Jimmy never lost when I was coaching him," was the only concession he allowed himself for the phenomenal contribution he made to Jimmy's success. In 1976 he published a book called *Pancho Segura's Championship Strategy*, with Gladys Heldman. In an interesting chapter at the end of the book entitled "Great Matches of Strategy," Pancho describes Connors versus Ashe and Connors versus Orantes, the two major matches Jimmy lost after Pancho's banishment. His old coach is admirably restrained in his analysis of how Connors lost them both. In the match against Ashe, Pancho merely says, "I wasn't in England, so saw the match on television," before launching into a critique of Connors's play. In the Orantes match, Pancho writes, "If I could have talked to Connors on the odd games in his match against Orantes, I would have told him to come to the net more to cut off the soft balls and to break up Orantes's rhythm. He could have come in more often on serve." Alas, Pancho was never again to be allowed to give Connors the benefit of his advice.

But 1975, that extraordinary year, with its fabulous highs and dismal lows, would never be forgotten. Watching his star student fall apart was very painful for the teacher. "Jimmy lost a lot of confidence that year," Pancho told Joel Drucker. "He was a great player, but we knew there were things he needed to go do get better. But the mother, oh, the mother. . . . I loved Jimbo, but what could I do?"

What he did was to go on coaching. He had other talented students, including Michael Chang, who came to live at La Costa so he could work with Pancho. Chang's small size and lack of power, plus his tenacity on the court and dedication to improving his game, reminded Pancho of his own youthful self, and the two worked well together for some time.

In 1993 Andre Agassi came to La Costa to see Pancho. The two knew each other, of course; Andre's sister was married to Pancho Gonzales, and the two Panchos had always stayed in touch. But if anyone thought this was going to be a replay of the great Segura-Connors partnership, they were to be disappointed. From the beginning, nothing went quite right. Agassi was overweight, a fact that Pancho found difficult to tolerate. His standards remained fiercely high, and if you could not get fit enough to play, Pancho was not interested. Moreover, Agassi had a sore wrist at the time, so was not in top form. Agassi lost in the first round of the U.S. Open that year and quickly abandoned his new coach. "I wish Andre had the guts to tell me he was out of shape then," Pancho told Joel Drucker, "With a little more patience and if his wrist had been healthy, we could have done so much." (Brad Gilbert then became Agassi's coach, and they had great success together.)

Desi Arnaz Jr. often visited his father in Del Mar and would go over to La Costa to see and play with his old coach. "By that time Pancho was a mythical figure," he recalled. "He had turned Jimmy Connors into a champion. He was wildly popular with the media. He invited all the celebrities to La Costa, the movie stars he had become friends with at the Beverly Hills Tennis Club. They all came down to La Costa to see him. La Costa was like Beverly Hills South. It was quite spectacular growing up in the tennis world at that time, and Pancho contributed hugely to that. He was legendary."

When Pancho left the Beverly Hills Tennis Club he took something with him—the spirit of fun, friendship, and flirtatiousness that he had brought to the club. It was never the same after that. Of course Spencer and his friends were no longer using the place as an after-school playpen. He and Dino were playing tennis for UCLA, along with the Kreiss brothers. Most of the others were in college or had jobs. So the group of kids that had given the place its energy and attraction were no longer going there. The movie people and their friends had also moved on. And Jimmy Connors, of course, was now in another league entirely.

As the Beverly Hills Tennis Club lost its main attraction, La Costa started to take off. Soon after Pancho arrived at Carlsbad, twenty-one tennis courts were added, the resort started an annual major tournament, the shop began to gross the highest figures of any tennis shop in the country, four assistant pros were hired to handle the influx of players, and La Costa was talked about as the greatest tennis mecca in the United States. Merv Adelson could hardly have foreseen the astuteness of his choice of tennis director. The tennis boom of the 1970s was in full swing, and Pancho was at the center of it.

Chapter Thirteen   Staying Loose at La Costa

Ever since his retirement from the pro tour, Pancho had continued to play competitive tennis. During the 1970s, there were some memorable matches, such as the one in Binghamton, New York, when Pancho, aged forty-six, reached the final, only to face Rod Laver, who had won his first Slam in 1962. Pancho lost to the twenty-nine-year-old champion, 6–4, 6–3. Not bad. Even better was a doubles match at the Jockey Club in Miami, between Pancho and his young protégé, Jimmy Connors, against Richard Gonzales and Ilie Nastase. It was a matchup made in heaven, and the crowd knew it. "We won!" Pancho recalled delightedly. "It was 12–10 in the third set. We played 102 percent and won!" It brought the house down.

In the summer of 1977, Pancho Segura and Pancho Gonzales entered the over-forty-five doubles tournament at Wimbledon. Segura was fifty-five years old, Gonzales was forty-eight. It was the centenary of the All England Lawn Tennis and Croquet Club Championship, and the president, Sir Brian Burnett, invited some of the great names in tennis to play in this special doubles event. They included Frank Sedgman, Bob Falkenberg, and Bobby Riggs, all former Wimbledon champions.

The two Panchos were to play the South African duo of Owen Williams and Abe Segal, the same Abe Segal who shared the record of playing the longest set ever played at Wimbledon against Segura and Olmedo in 1968. "We played on court fourteen, which had the biggest grandstand other than Centre Court," Owen Williams remembered. "It was the show court in those days. We were drawing the third biggest crowd at Wimbledon, and I hadn't played competitive tennis in fifteen years, so I was very nervous."

The four started playing, and Gonzales began fooling around. "He was hitting the ball behind his back," Owen recalled, "and looking one way and playing the perfect drop shot, while we scrambled. He toyed with us." But after they lost the first set, the two South Africans decided to change their tactics. "We can't do any worse than this," Abe said to his partner, "Let's just hit the hell out of the ball."

"So we blasted away," Owen said, "and somehow we won. Segoo wasn't playing very well that day, I'm not sure why. Anyway, we won the match. Look, they had ten years on us. We had only just turned forty-five. Segura took it very well, but Gonzales hardly shook hands with us afterwards."

Owen Williams said later that although it was his moment of glory, he was sad to have beaten these men, who were his heroes. "I had modeled my game after Gonzales. There was something bittersweet about beating him, because he didn't like it."

During the match, however, there were some lighter moments between the two old warriors. Gordon Forbes, Abe Segal's former tennis partner, was watching the match with thousands of other "nostalgic spectators," as he put it. He described in his memoir the following exchange between the two Panchos:

> A Segal forehand flies down the middle of the court, leaving both [Gonzales] and Segura standing.
> "Your ball, keed," says Pancho Segura.
> "I tell you what we do, Sneaky," says Pancho Gonzales. "You *watch* the ball and I *hit* it, okay?"

There were dozens of asides like this, Forbes said. The fans were delighted.

Little Pancho would never lose that crowd-pleasing magic on the court. His talent was to take that magic and use it throughout the later part of his working life. And at La Costa he was well rewarded for his gift. "I rob the rich and get to keep it!" he joked. "I'm a Latino Robin Hood!" In 1980 he and Beverley built a handsome ranch house that backed on to the La Costa grounds. It had a pool and a lovely garden, a country-style family room and kitchen with a cathedral ceiling, and a study for the coach with photographs on the walls of Pancho's tennis history.

Throughout the decade of the seventies, La Costa was at its most successful. Davis Cup matches were played there. Celebrity tournaments took place there. A special stadium was built so the matches could be watched and televised properly. Beverley loved being at La Costa. "I enjoyed running the shop," she said, "and being on the grounds of the resort all the time. There was very little going on in Carlsbad then. Pancho and I were stars. All the movie people came down to visit us. Friends called us 'Chocolate and Vanilla.'" (Perhaps that was inspired in part by Pancho's nickname for his wife, "Yum.") "It was also wonderful for a child growing up there," Beverley added. "It was Maria's backyard. Everyone looked out for her."

By this time most of Segura's Guayaquil family had come to live in the United States, thanks to the generosity of the golden boy, brother Pancho. They would visit him at La Costa and see him in his luxurious surroundings, with beautiful people walking about the grounds in expensive clothes. They would gape at the lavish landscapes with fountains and swoon over his elegant house. "He would feed them and have them to stay, and all they did was complain," Beverley said. "He did everything for them. He tried to get them an education, sending them books, telling them where to enroll in college. They still complain. They think he owes them a living, and yet he did so much for them."

Spencer also liked going to La Costa. "I would go on the weekends," he explained.

Here's what my routine was. I'd wake up in the morning and play some tennis. They had pretty good pros. Then I'd go to lunch with my dad every day. And he was doing what he always did, teaching eight, nine, ten hours a day, with good juniors like Michael Chang. It was slow at first, because La Costa was in the middle of nowhere and it only had four tennis courts. But after a while, the place became famous and everyone flocked to my dad. "I'm going down to see my good friend Pancho and hang out with him," they'd say. We'd eat lunch, play two more hours, then I'd go to the spa, have my massage. Then we'd have a drink and go to bed.

That was when Spencer was still playing serious tennis. He was the captain of the UCLA tennis team in 1974, his senior year, and La Costa was where he practiced and worked out with his father. For when Spencer started playing good tennis, his father began to take a serious interest. Spencer might become a champion after all. "He didn't spend time with me when I was young, but all of a sudden when I became a good tennis player he wanted to spend a ton of time with me. But there was too much pressure."

Spencer's emergence as a tennis player contained the seeds of disaster. "I first beat my dad when I was eighteen. Then he beat me right back. He was very competitive, always. And me? I didn't really want to beat him. All I wanted to do was please him."

Psychiatrists would have a field day with that revealing confession. To have a famous and adored father, a hungry young son, and a game they both played competitively: nobody could have worked through that without some suffering.

The fact was that Spencer didn't really want to compete. And yet he was on a tennis court playing opponents against whom competitiveness could make the difference between winning and losing. His emotions would get the better of him. "I would play better and better, but then I wanted to lose because I didn't want to be better than my dad. It was very frustrating. I had matches where I would be up 6–0, 4–0, against a number ten player in the world, and then fall apart. I would serve twenty aces and then find a way to lose. I was always playing three people—my dad, my opponent, and myself."

For a while, Pancho worked hard with Spencer at La Costa, realizing that he could be as good as the top players on the circuit.

"Play harder, play harder," he would urge his son. But the conflict was always there. "I wanted to be number one, and yet I would never compete with my dad. So I would lose and feel terrible. I had the confidence of a butterfly."

Spencer's seesaw tennis career took its toll. After leaving UCLA, he moved into an apartment in Brentwood, where Desi, Dino, and Jimmy Connors would drop in from time to time. Spencer dated movie stars—celebrities' daughters, like Lisa Todd (whom he dated for a few years after meeting her at Wimbledon)—and played tennis. He played for a full season after leaving college, with Pancho on his back, as tough and unforgiving as he had once been with himself. Pancho was not going to give his son any slack. He would say, "Yes, I will come and watch you—but only if you win!" Once Spencer called him from a tournament and said, "Dad, it's really hot. It's 120 degrees and it's really not fun to play out there." His father immediately shot back, "But it's also 120 degrees for the other guy!"

Spencer won a round in the Australian Open, lost in the first round at the French, and lost in the last qualifying round for Wimbledon, meanwhile acquiring a computer ranking of 182 in the world. But he watched his own tennis game continue to struggle as Jimmy's soared. "I can't go on doing this," Spencer said. His volatile talent, vying with suppressed anger, expressed itself in increasingly erratic ways on the tennis court. In 1975, emotionally drained and frustrated, he quit the professional game.

Pancho was not quite ready to let his son leave the sport he loved. After Spencer quit tennis, he went to Loyola Law School. One weekend his freshman year, he went down to La Costa with a girlfriend, and Pancho ran up to him and said, "You're playing." Spencer said, "Dad, I'm not playing, I'm in law school." Pancho insisted, "You're playing." It turned out Pancho had been betting with Bobby Riggs, a regular visitor to La Costa, and was down five hundred dollars. Pancho then bet Riggs that Spencer would beat him—five hundred dollars, winner take all. The veteran champion agreed, but on the condition that Spencer not come to the net.

So Spencer had to go on to the tennis court and face Bobby Riggs, for his father's honor. "I was terrified to have to rally with Bobby Riggs," Spencer said, "because he was so great at the baseline. But I had a really huge serve, and in the end I beat him. My big serve started the pace, and he couldn't keep up." The story had a typical Pancho ending: it was not Spencer who got any of the five hundred dollars for winning, but Pancho. He gave his courageous son a token sum for his effort. The pressure, however, cost Spencer a good deal more.

Riggs and Segura regularly played doubles together, with Riggs still finding ways to exploit the "Battle of the Sexes" financial bonanza he had enjoyed in 1975, thanks to Billie Jean King. In 1981 and 1982, Pancho and Bobby played two pairs of female professionals for a fairly substantial box-office take.

If Spencer could not in the end reap the benefit of Pancho's guidance, other players took his son's place as new tennis hopes during the coach's years at La Costa. Viktoria Beggs was a young player whose sister, Alexi, had come to work as Pancho's assistant at La Costa in 1979. Vikki was on the tour at the time, and Pancho became interested in her. He also found out that she had graduated from the University of Miami, Pancho's alma mater, and in no time the two became friends. "I was there one week, visiting Alexi," Vikki remembered, "and Pancho watched me with the players at the club, and he would stand behind me and tell me what to do, and then I went back on the tour and started winning all my matches! After one week with Pancho!"

Vikki began to return regularly to La Costa over the next few years, to inhale some of Pancho's wisdom. "My most vivid experience there was when Pancho told me to play a man who had come down to La Costa to rejuvenate in the spa. He had played in the juniors and was a very good player, and Pancho told me, 'You're going to play Max (not his real name), and you're going to give him the alleys, and you're going to give him 15–love in the game score, and I'm going to put up five thousand dollars, and so are some of my friends, that you win.'" (The same trick he had worked on Jimmy Connors at the Beverly Hills Tennis Club!)

Vikki went on to the court and waited to return serve, thinking about all the money Pancho was risking on her. "I was shaking so badly, my racket was virtually doing figure eights, so I think, okay, just pretend this is how you return serve. So I battle, battle, battle, because he had 15–love and the alleys. What that did was make me focus dramatically on the first few points of every game, because I couldn't afford to let him get ahead. The first set was a pure battle, and in the end I won 7–5. The second set was a little bit easier."

After her victory, Vikki watched Pancho and his friends divide up the money. (She later learned that Max was not playing for the cash. Max was playing for something quite different. Pancho had outrageously promised him that she would "put out" for him if she lost. "Thank goodness you didn't tell me that!" Vikki exclaimed. "I wouldn't have been able to play at all!") The fact that Pancho had told her how much money he was betting on her made Vikki play her best. "That stayed with me," she said. "When I went back out to play the girls on tour, I wasn't nervous at all because there's something about playing for someone else's money, and especially someone you respect and admire, that makes you stretch yourself to the limit not to let him down. His technique gave you a laser focus."

Vikki later went back to school and earned a degree as a sports psychologist. She is now a tennis coach herself. She says that most of the techniques she teaches she learned from Pancho. "For example, if you play a player deep into the corner, virtually they have only two zones to which they can respond, depending on their capability. They might play defense or they might go down the line. Going crosscourt is impossible—geometrically impossible. So Pancho would scream, 'There's no other way! There's no other place they can go!'"

Vikki's students learn to analyze a player's grip, to tell what type of shot they could potentially hit. "Everyone tells you to watch the ball," she goes on, "but Pancho defined it much more elaborately."

You're watching the ball in relation to your opponent's body. Is the ball close to the player's body? Is the ball far away from the player's body? Is the ball in front of the player's body? All those three positionings will determine what kind of shot the player is going to give back to you. If the player disguises his shot, you watch the ball clear the net. The higher it clears the net, the deeper it will land. The shorter it clears the net, the closer in it will land. So now you know exactly what kind of shot is coming to you, and you can virtually saunter over there. You are just waiting, waiting in the zone of this spin, this speed, for the ball to come to you. All these principles, of analysis, of anticipation, I learned from Pancho.

The powerful effects of these lessons sparked in Vikki a new passion for the game. "Once I had these principles ingrained in me, it became just a pleasure. I was laughing to myself, "Oh, yes! They're going to hit there, there. . . . And then I'll hit this." With Vicky's psychological expertise, other aspects of Pancho's genius as a teacher earned her particular respect.

Pancho taught the score. He was brilliant at making you understand that you don't squander the point if you don't have to. You wait your time and maybe you have to rework everything to get them on the run. If you don't know the score, you're going to give some points away because you aren't making your best shot selection, which means when you're down, you play your high percentage shots until you see an opening.

The beauty of Pancho's approach is the confidence he would give you. Everyone has a weakness and/or a strength. But if you can nullify their strength, they get frustrated. Everyone has keys to their play, and you just have to keep looking and figuring it out until you understand them. Another thing I learned from Pancho is that there is no time limit to a tennis match. If one strategy isn't working, you can come up with another and another, and as long as you have the stamina, you can go on forever.

That was always one of Pancho's pet peeves—it's shameful to lose a match because you're not fit. That was his peeve with Andre that year—he wasn't even trying to get fit. The irony is that later Andre became very fit working with Brad Gilbert, and I think Pancho really inspired him to get that way.

Countless other players came away from La Costa playing better tennis after a few hours with Pancho. He was that good. Even when he slowed down, with his bandy-legs even bandier, he never lost his skills. "I remember going to La Costa and seeing this old man who moved in jerky waddling movements with his bowlegs," recalled a businessman from New York, "and I stood on the baseline, thinking this would be absurdly easy, and I could not get a ball back—not one! He anticipated everything with total accuracy!" Pancho could still run his opponents back and forth like a windshield wiper with the fiendish precision of his game.

During the early years at La Costa, Pancho spent a lot of time playing in celebrity tournaments around the world, traveling in private jets with friends like billionaire Kirk Kerkorian, who was a longtime admirer. "Neither of us had much to start with," Kerkorian said recently. "Our backgrounds were similar. We both made it to the top, me from Armenia, Pancho from Ecuador. I admire him very much. Such a masterful player and always so upbeat."

Pancho enjoyed the excitement of the success of La Costa and the wealthy clients who played with him, who were entertained by his salacious stories and who invited him to their mansions at home and abroad. By this time he was completely comfortable with celebrities, however rich or important they were. Spencer remembered picking up the phone in the La Costa office to hear Diana Ross on the other end, asking for a tennis lesson. "He says he's never to be disturbed when he's teaching, no call, nothing. But they page him because it's Diana Ross. I say to him, 'Dad, Diana Ross is on the phone.' He yells furiously at me, 'I don't care who it is!' He is angry at me because they page him for Diana Ross!"

One year he bought a bright red Thunderbird. "I was around young people all the time," he said in explanation. "That made me feel young. It was a fireman's car! A banana car! I was the talk of the town, everyone thought I was nuts. But I was happy because I was teaching, and tennis was in fashion then." His daughter, Maria, said she was so embarrassed by it that when he took her to school she made him drop her off around the corner.

By the 1990s, Pancho had been coaching for over thirty years, and the pace of La Costa had slowed considerably. As with so many institutions depending on fashion for their survival, La Costa in its later years lost its bloom. Other resorts sprang up, focusing more on golf, which had overtaken tennis as the most popular leisure sport for the rich. In 1987, La Costa was purchased by a Japanese company, Sports Shinko, for $250 million, and the show-biz glamour that Merv Adelson and his friends had brought to the place disappeared. Visitors to La Costa after that were more business people than celebrities—lawyers, corporate executives, venture capitalists—just as rich, but less splashy.

Beverley also stopped going to La Costa, except sometimes for lunch. She quit working in the shop and more or less retired to the house she had so lovingly decorated. She found traveling more and more wearisome, having been spoiled by the luxurious private transportation they had enjoyed in La Costa's heyday. Their daughter, Maria, married and divorced and returned to live nearby with her young son, another reason to stay close to home.

Pancho continued to teach. Tennis, after all, was his life. Dr. Abraham Verghese, a professor of medicine in Texas and published author, wrote about his time with Pancho at La Costa with the affection and awe that Pancho could still arouse as a coach (see the excerpt from his memoir *The Tennis Partner* in the appendix to this book).

But Pancho, with all his energy and charm, began to overstep the mark sometimes with the people who had once appreciated him most of all—women. His characteristic racy humor and saucy stories began to lose their timing. They started to raise eyebrows, not laughter. They were no longer sexy, but in the language of the time, sexist.

A young, New York fashion writer, who was a keen tennis player and also very good-looking, came to take lessons from Pancho at La Costa in the late 1980s. Her experience, probably shared by more than one female guest, was not something she would ever wish to repeat. Pancho set up her up to take a lesson with a visiting businessman, and then, in front of him, said that he, Pancho, would play her and if he won, he would demand from her essentially what he had promised that Max would get from Vikki Beggs if he won—her sexual favors. If she won a game off him—one game—she could have whatever warm-up suit she wanted from the pro shop.

Upset and embarrassed, the young woman went on the court to play. She played better than she had ever played, but she could not get a point off him. Not one point, let alone a game. "You're really good," Pancho said afterward. He did not demand she fulfill her side of the bargain. Of course not. He was only teasing. He was only being Pancho. They played again after that, and it was as though nothing untoward had ever been said. Much later, Pancho saw the young woman at the U.S. Open and greatly impressed her by remembering her, saying, "You're the writer from New York." For him, it had been a harmless encounter.

Jean Longacre, former manager of the Beverly Hills Tennis Club, noted that when she asked previous members for any stories they remembered about Pancho, Ed Hookstratten, a former president of the club, replied, "They're all dirty." Pancho's personality was bound up in those routines he had learned from stand-up comedians and gag writers over the years, abetted by his own typical Latino's enthusiasm for sexual innuendo. But remarks taken in stride in the forgiving sixties at the Beverly Hills Tennis Club were no longer so readily acceptable in the politically correct climate of the eighties and nineties.

Friends heard rumors of his peccadilloes at La Costa and laughed, knowing the innocence of their perpetrator. But the

Japanese management perhaps heard just one too many reports about these little exchanges from unamused guests. Pancho's lewd comments and naughty jokes, particularly coming now from a much older man to younger women, fell on very different ears at La Costa, and his increasingly risqué comments came back to haunt him. Skating on very thin ice, in the end he was punished for the very characteristics that had made him so beloved in earlier days.

There were other warning signs of mortality. In 1995, Pancho was at Wimbledon when he learned that his old comrade and rival, Pancho Gonzales, was dying. Gonzales's later life had been sad. His marriage to Rita Agassi was over, although she had given him a son, Skylar, whom he loved. He lost his invaluable endorsement deal with Spalding in 1981, and left Caesars Palace in 1985, after sixteen years, shortly after Cliff Perlman, his sponsor and supporter, left. Gonzales lived out his final years in Las Vegas, mostly by himself, as he had always been throughout his life, living in a modest cottage, sleeping on a mattress on the floor, a lone wolf to the last. He was diagnosed with stomach and esophageal cancer in 1994, when he was sixty-six years old.

Gonzales fought the cancer as he had fought on the tennis court. He had always hated to lose. In June 1995, he went into the hospital in Las Vegas, and when Wimbledon started, he tried to watch the matches on TV. The effort didn't last long. He died on July 3, in the middle of the tournament. Pancho Segura didn't leave Wimbledon to go to Las Vegas for the funeral. "I couldn't get a reservation," he explained. In fact, he admitted later, he couldn't face it. The two Panchos talked on the phone one last time, on the great player's deathbed. "You want money, Gorgo?" Little Pancho asked. "I'll take care of it. I'll send you anything you want." As it turned out, it wasn't necessary. Gonzales died with his usual finely tuned sense of timing, during one of the semifinal rounds of the tournament where he had been such a legendary player for so long. Andre Agassi paid for the funeral.

Three months later, on October 25, 1995, Bobby Riggs died

of cancer at the age of seventy-seven. As described in Tom LeCompte's biography of Riggs, *The Last Sure Thing*, Pancho, along with Jack Kramer and Ted Schroeder attended the memorial service five days later. "He kept me in a state of alertness," Pancho told the mourners. "He taught me how to play poker and gin rummy when we were on tour and working for three hundred dollars a week, and I had no money coming to me. It was fun." Pancho also said about Riggs's tennis game, "He could make the ball talk."

So many of Pancho's old tennis friends died too soon—Lew Hoad, aged fifty-nine, Arthur Ashe, Ellsworth Vines, Fred Perry. Others retired with injuries. Meanwhile, Jimmy Connors had stopped playing, after several years on the senior tour, and had retired from tennis, never attending any of the big championships or appearing in public in support of the game he had loved and transformed. While his successors—Nastase, Borg, Becker, McEnroe, Sampras, Agassi, and many others, moved in and out of the Grand Slam spotlight, Pancho seemed immortal, playing on into his seventies and eighties. "I want to be like him when I grow up," commented his old University of Miami coach and legendary champion Gardnar Mulloy, at the age of ninety-two.

In 2001, the Japanese decided not to renew Pancho's contract. The club was beginning to lose money, and the Shinko Corporation sold it to KSL Resorts later that year for $120 million, taking a large loss. The resort now is being redeveloped as a mixed community of condominium units and a large hotel for conventions and business meetings, providing golf and tennis on the side.

Pancho retired shortly after the new century began, a still-active and enthusiastic proponent of the game to which he had devoted himself for seventy-five years.

By the 1980s, awards and accolades began to roll in. Pancho was inducted into the Newport Tennis Hall of Fame in 1984, memorialized forever as the first person to make the two-handed forehand not only acceptable but one of the most effective shots in the game. One of his many other awards, given by the Association of Tennis Professionals, reads: "His skill, spirit, and enthusiasm helped professional tennis survive its darkest days. As a teacher of tennis, he has few peers. As a player, he was a virtuoso. As a man he is the friend of all who love this game."

In 1988, at the age of sixty-seven, Pancho Segura won the Huggy Bears Championship, a tournament started in 1985 in Long Island by eight teams of friends and local pros. It soon expanded into a major charity tennis event every summer that attracted some of the best doubles players in the game, with the money raised going to disadvantaged children all over the world. Pancho played that year with Paul Annacone against Anand Amritraj and Wally Masur, the latter pair much younger, and with several titles to their credit. Their skills were no match for the sixty-seven-year-old maestro, who stunned them all.

Inspired by this victory, the Huggy Bears organizers, Tony, Theodore, and Nicholas Forstmann, created the Pancho Segura Award for his extraordinary performance that day. "Pancho epitomized the words 'team player,' the way he meshed with Paul to secure that victory," the program notes recorded. Later winners of the award were singled out for their brilliant doubles partnering.

Friends began to think up more lasting memorials to Pancho's greatness. Vic Braden made a video with him and Jack Kramer (70 Minutes with Big Jake and Pancho). "I didn't want people not to know how great they were," Braden said. He recalled the early days when he played with Pancho. "Right from the beginning, you could see that he almost had a love affair with the tennis ball. You could see how he nurtured the ball. And everybody loved him."

Another tennis legend has recently surfaced to record Pancho's greatness, completely surprising the tennis world. His name is Jimmy Connors. After all those years of estrangement, something wonderful happened. Pancho began to get the credit, finally, for his years of work with the controversial champion. In the last few years Jimmy Connors has started doing commentary for the BBC at Wimbledon, and in 2005 he said over the airwaves—for millions to hear—the following: "I don't think anyone knew more about the game than Pancho Segura. . . . I needed to be around a male influence and he was certainly that to me."

When he said that, Jimmy was watching a match between Sebastien Grosjean and Andy Roddick. At one point as the match progressed, Jimmy commented on the air, "Now Grosjean, on Roddick's second serve, *should move in and take a chance.*" Pancho's very words! All those years later, Jimmy was instinctively echoing Pancho's own advice to his pupil. "In my career," Jimmy went on, "that's one thing I wish I'd done more, take a chance on the second serve." If Pancho had heard that, how he would have grinned with delight—the coach's classic principle served up by his greatest student.

In recent years in the Players Lounge at Wimbledon, people steal a glance at Jimmy and his former coach sitting down together, talking tennis, just like old times, as though no silence (or mother) had ever separated them. ("I believe in JC," Pancho jokes to the fans who come up to shake his hand. "Jimmy Connors!") Jimmy's position is clear: "My generation—anybody who was around tennis—would say, 'There goes Pancho Segura.' There's nothing but the utmost respect for his attitude, for his game, his abilities as a coach and just overall."

But at the U.S. Open in 2006, a new twist in the Jimmy Connors story emerged. People noticed that Connors was appearing in public at a tournament he had often shunned. He looked older, of course, with lines, wearing spectacles at times, but the angry, reclusive Jimmy Connors of the past was suddenly center stage again, after all those years. He had agreed earlier that summer to coach Andy Roddick, the talented but flawed hope of American tennis. After a great start, Roddick had struggled over the past year (losing in a humiliating straight-sets loss to Britain's Andy Murray in the third round at Wimbledon), and even changing coaches had not helped him win the major tournaments.

Enter Jimmy Connors.

In the 2006 U.S. Open, Roddick played better than anyone had seen him play all year, getting beaten in four sets in the final by the almost-impossible-to-beat Grand Slam hero Roger Federer. Everybody knew why Roddick had gotten so far. He moved better on the court, he was more aggressive, he waited for the short ball, he came to the net and put the ball away. In short, Jimmy was teaching him to play the Connors game. And who had taught Jimmy to play his game? Pancho Segura. It was clear what was going on—*Andy Roddick was learning Pancho Segura's skills via Jimmy Connors, and they were working.* Thus a great teacher passes on his knowledge down through the generations. (Later, Roddick changed coaches again but still failed to beat Federer, losing to him in the semifinals of the 2009 Australian Open under new coach Larry Stefanki.)

Spencer Segura saw Connors at the Open. In spite of Pancho's long drought with the Connors family, Spencer had remained in touch over the years. With a daughter from his second marriage, he now has a third wife, Amanda, and a baby boy, Spencer Francisco II. Jimmy Connors is the boy's godfather.

Spencer's romance with tennis took a nosedive after those early years. He finished law school and temporarily became a lawyer, with entertainment clients such as Joan Collins. "I was like an agent," he said, "but it was not what I wanted." Later he went into real estate, and then Wall Street. One of his partners was Theodore (Teddy) Forstmann, who helped run the Huggy Bears tournament.

Forstmann persuaded Spencer to play serious tennis again, and the two became doubles partners, winning several tournaments.

In 1977 Spencer played with his father in the USTA Father-Son Indoor Tennis Championship in Houston, Texas. They won the tournament, a classic moment of glory for the two Seguras. "I learned how to play competitively from playing with great players who were friends of my father's," Spencer said later. "That's what I loved. And my father taught you to be competitive by making you laugh as you learned."

Quarrels are over, friends move on, but a tennis player like Pancho never stops playing tennis. He may not lift a tennis racket much, but in his head he is still on the court, watching, thinking, stroking the ball, returning serve, waiting like a panther to strike, to make the killer drop shot. "I grew up with nothing except my tennis racket and my character," he said. In his later years, nothing would change that assessment. He sometimes dreams of games he has played in the past. A few come back to haunt him. "I lost a match to Jack Kramer in Santa Barbara. I had him 5–love, 5–1. I had him that time, and lost 8–6 in the end. I dream of that sometimes." Another Kramer match looms in his mind during a sleepless night. "In London I had him 4–2 in the fifth set, and he beat me. I was just coming up and he was the star, and he thought I was not capable of playing that sort of tennis. He had size on me, big game, big overhead, big serve, his backhand was better than mine, but I moved very quickly, better than him, and that surprised him. The only matches you hate to lose are those you are in a position of winning. That loss affected me for two or three days."

Some of his dreams are of games he never played. "I dreamed I was playing doubles with Gonzales and he was insulting me. An overhead was hit to us and he said, 'Let me have that overhead!'"

Jack Kramer, the man most often in Pancho's dreams, who played the most important role of all in Pancho's early career as a professional, and who helped bring the sport to millions by keeping it alive until the open era, knows better than anyone how much his old colleague on the tour contributed to the game of tennis. "Pancho has never gotten anywhere near the recognition or the credit he deserves in helping the popularity of the sport grow, not just in America but all over the world, because even though he was not the best player, he was certainly the most popular player. He was one of the saviors of the sport."

"Pancho turned pro too early," observes Peter Bodo of *Tennis Magazine*. "I understand why, but it meant he could not compete in the Grand Slam tournaments until the pros were invited in 1968, by which time he was too old for a title. But not winning any of the four Slams—the Australian, the French, Wimbledon, the U.S. Open—means that he does not appear in any of the major stats about the greatest players of the time. This is very unfair, since, like Gonzales, he undoubtedly was one."

Pancho's devotion to the game that made him what he is will never fade. He continues to attend the big matches in Europe and the United States. Not only the big ones but Indian Wells and Key Biscayne, any tennis event he can reasonably get to. As always, when the TV cameras pan over the audience, looking for famous faces, they always linger on Pancho, unmistakable with his dark skin and shock of white hair, usually grinning at some x-rated joke that luckily the television audience cannot hear.

If he can't get to the tournaments, he watches tennis avidly on TV, following the new talents, recalling the old, analyzing, criticizing, encouraging, always fixed on the game he loves. "He's just a great fan," Jack Kramer says. "He loves to be around tennis and he will never stop loving it as long as he lives."

Pancho is invited by acquaintances to help coach their children. Some parents, ambitious like Gloria Connors, hope that some of Pancho's wisdom will rub off on their hard-driven, athletic young boys and girls who dream of being Roger Federer or Maria Sharapova. Most of them do not have the hunger or commitment to get there. Pancho, of all people, knows how much it takes. He is the wise man of tennis.

California, 2005. Pancho is watching a teenage girl hit balls to her coach on a private court near San Diego. He watches her like a lynx, noting her stance, her footwork, her position on the court. His observations come pouring out.

"The forehand is a better shot for you because you can run around it."

"Bend your knees for more extension and more momentum."

"More cross-court—penetrate deep—then back it up by coming to the net."

"Get a little lower! Get low!"

"Be patient. Wait for the short ball. Be patient!"

At the end he goes up to her, smiling.

"Attagirl, baby! That's the way to play tennis! Who plays better than you?" There is a pause. "'*Nobody*.' That's what I want to hear you say."

Later, the girl's mother takes Pancho aside and tells him her daughter has injured her shoulder and a tournament is coming up. What should they do?

"She must play if she wants to play," Pancho replies. "Go by what she says. But then, if she plays, no excuses."

He explains later that if he were coaching her, he would not let her play. "The injury puts a hindrance in her mind. If she loses, she can then use it as an excuse, and in the future, psychologically that excuse will help her lose. These discussions with her mother about whether to play are bad for her, making her lose confidence. Parents are never a help to a coach."

Ecuador, 2005. Pancho goes back to Guayaquil with his son, Spencer, and new daughter-in-law, Amanda. It is a triumphal return. As one of the greatest athletes Ecuador has ever produced, he is greeted with honor by Ecuadorian athletic leaders such as Danilo Carrera Drouet and Efren Cherrez, the president and general secretary of the Ecuador Olympic Committee. Television cameras follow him around; journalists interview him; he is showered with medals and awards at grand luncheons and taken to the most exclusive men's clubs for dinner.

In the huge ballroom of the Union Club in Guayaquil, a magnificent room of carved wood moldings and high windows, Pancho sits alone, unobserved for a moment, in a vast, leather, wing chair. The image is very powerful: this small, dark-skinned man with a mane of white hair, who as a child could never in a million years have stepped foot across the threshold of this grand building, now welcomed here as a conquering hero. It's almost unimaginable how far he has traveled from the old Guayaquil Tennis Club, where day after day the undernourished kid watched his father work, from time to time picking up a tennis racket and hitting the ball over and over in a kind of hopeful dream. Sitting by himself all these years later in the hushed silence of Guayaquil's Union Club ballroom, distant for a moment from the noise and adulation of the crowds, he is still at heart that skinny little ball boy from the barrio, gazing at the Grace Line ships sailing off to a golden destination forever beyond his reach.

One morning during the visit, Pancho takes a tennis clinic with Ecuador's young up-and-coming talent, seducing them with his naughty jokes and colorful comments. Although unable to move much, in many cases he can show vital elements of strategy with his racket and his position on the court. The coach of these aspiring young talents is Miguel Olvera, who played on the winning Ecuador Davis Cup Team in 1969. "I learned everything from Pancho," he acknowledges.

Old and young people wave to him, "Hola, Pancho!" heads sticking out of the windows of buses, groups staring out of shop doors, recognizing without difficulty this small wiry man with his white hair, bright eyes, bandy-legs, big grins, as he hobbles slowly down the crowded streets. He makes off-the-cuff remarks that are as bawdy and blush-making as ever. The locals will never stop loving him.

He is honored at a celebration lunch at the Guayaquil Tennis Club, with the club's president, Antonio Sola, many former luminaries of the game, and dignitaries of the Ecuador Olympic Committee in attendance. The club is much bigger now, with many more courts, all clay now instead of cement. But some things remain the same. As lunch is served, on the nearby courts ball boys run about chasing balls for the club members as they play their midday games. "We help the ball boys now," Antonio Sola confides, "hoping, hoping someone will come up. But there'll never be another Segura."

Another extraordinary lunch has been arranged at the Annexe Tennis Club, a splendidly landscaped facility, where he meets, after more years than he cares to count, members of the Bruckmann Burton family who whisked him off to Quito in 1937 when, as an undernourished little boy, he first began to show his promise. One of the sisters to whom he had taught tennis, Ilse Bruckmann Breihl de Orrantia, sits in stately splendor at the lunch table with her daughter, Maria. She is a beautiful old lady now, elegantly dressed, with a twinkle in her eye. Pancho immediately rushes to greet her. He eagerly sits next to her, and they start exchanging confidences in Spanish like the young teenagers they once were. The nostalgia is palpable. At one moment he says something naughty and she blushes and laughs, murmuring, "Panchito, Panchito, *igual que siempre!*" ("The same as always!")

Pancho has one more visit to make. This one is not so easy. His eighty-year-old sister still lives in the house where he was born, and he makes his way to the green-painted building on the corner of Cuenca and Quito streets with a mixture of anger and sadness, knowing too well what will greet him there. A large number of family members (some he doesn't even know) are impatiently assembled in the small, hot, humid, living space over the shuttered store. There is hardly any furniture. Faded photographs of their legendary relative hang crookedly on the moldy, peeling walls. Wires are strung from a tiny television to naked light bulbs. Pancho does not look around, does not point out his shabby old room, averts his eyes from the miserable slum of a kitchen.

He sits down at the table in the center of the room and his family crowd around him, peppering him with questions, requests, rattling off demands to him in rapid Spanish, thrusting dirty scraps of paper at him that he must read, explain, sign. "The telephone is cut off. We need your signature to get it on again." They finger him, stroke him, caress him, as though his stardust will rub off on them, as though their physical connection to him will somehow magically ease their troubles. Pancho is their miracle, their treasure, the goose that laid the golden egg, the one who succeeded beyond anyone's wildest dreams, the one who got away.

They look at him with awe, smile at him, touch him, ask him for autographs, for friends, for children, for anyone. ("I sent them a big new TV, but it was stolen," Pancho whispers, sighing.) He signs photographs, he talks, he tells stories, he laughs, he tells more stories, he peels notes from a wad of dollars and hands it to them. Then he gets up, disentangling himself, eager to be gone. The embraces and torrents of farewell messages last several minutes.

When Pancho leaves, he is no longer wearing his signature, white warm-up jacket. It is now wrapped around the shoulders of a cousin, who smiles and waves good-bye, clutching the jacket, proud of his new acquisition and the status it gives him. Pancho looks back one last time, then climbs into the waiting car.

He'll never forget what he said so long ago after his coach Gardnar Mulloy told him what it would take to become a great tennis player: "If it weren't for tennis I'd be chasing alligators with all the other Indians in swimming pools in Miami." The Inca Warrior laughs his infectious laugh at this undeniable truth and then adds, with the same energy and passion he brought to the game, "I was happy all my life because I was doing what I loved."

Acknowledgments

From the beginning, Pancho Segura opened his heart to me about his colorful life, drawing upon an astonishing memory going back over eighty years, with a candor and wit that have marked his personality throughout his long career. My time with him was beyond price. (He even agreed to hit a few tennis balls with me, so that I could tell my children I played tennis with the great Pancho Segura!) His son, Spencer, while speaking very candidly about his own life as well as his father's, opened his Rolodex, giving me names, places, suggestions, and access to people whom I could not possibly have reached otherwise. His patience, when I asked him for yet another name or phone number, was exemplary. The rest of Pancho's family were equally helpful in describing their background in Ecuador, and what it was like to be related to a tennis legend.

Beverley Segura talked to me about the early days of her marriage and the tour with great honesty and humor. Virginia Giesbert was most hospitable with her time and memories, and allowed me to make use of her wonderful collection of photographs. Jean Longacre at the Beverly Hills Tennis Club used up hours of her valuable time getting in touch with members who might have memories of Pancho, and allowed me to spend a delightful day at the club meeting and interviewing them. Greg Gonzales was extraordinarily generous in sharing with me the large archive, including unpublished material, about his uncle, Richard Gonzales. Lornie Kuhle, James Lichtman, and Sridhar Srinivasan all helped me in various important ways during the writing of the book.

In particular I'd like to thank Jimmy Connors, who, after many years of avoiding interviews and preferring privacy and seclusion to the glare of the celebrity sports spotlight, generously talked to me for the greater part of a day about his life and tennis career.

In Guayaquil, Ecuador, Danilo Carrera Drouet, president of the Ecuador Olympic Committee, Dr. Efren Cherrez, general secretary of the committee, Antonio Sola, president of the Guayaquil Tennis Club, and Nicolas Lapentti and Diego Ante, were all enormously hospitable during my visit there. I'd also like to thank Mario Canesso Oneto, for the gift of his marvelous book, *100 Años de Historia del Tenis Ecuatoriano* (parts of which were helpfully translated for me by Princeton University graduate student Freddy Dominguez), and to Alberto Sanchez for sending me a compact disc of Pancho's memorabilia at the exhibition in his honor in Guayaquil in 2005.

Pancho is particularly grateful to the All England Lawn Tennis Club chairman, Tim Phillips, and the British Lawn Tennis Association CEO, John Crowther, for their generosity over the years, as well as to Christian Bimes, president of the French Tennis Federation, Geoff Pollard, president of Tennis Australia, and Alan G. Schwartz and Franklin R. Johnson, former and current presidents of the United States Tennis Association.

Many other people helped me along the way, with memories, photographs, anecdotes, wisdom, and insights. They include: Desi Arnaz Jr., Henry Bamberger, Viktoria Beggs, David Blum, Peter Bodo, Vic Braden, Ilse Bruckmann Breihl, Butch Buchholz, Stan Canter, Manuel Carrera del Rio, Joel Drucker, Ron Dunas, Carl Earn, Joan Emery, Catherine Ettlinger, Mike Franks, John Hall, Jennifer Hoad, Ed Hookstratten, Elvira Karam, Kirk Kerkorian, Travis Kleefeld, Jack Kramer, Don Kreiss, Tom Kreiss, Rod Laver, Jeanne Martin, Gardnar Mulloy, Alex Olmedo, Miguel Olvera, Maria Orrantia Bruckmann, Cliff Perlman, Kay Pick, Ronald A. Recht, Robert Rosenkranz, Ken Rosewall, Abe Segal, Stan Smith, Joseph B. Stahl, Dr. Abraham Verghese, Rosalind Walter, David White, Owen Williams, and Carmita Zafman.

I should add my thanks to all my friends at the Bucks County Racquet Club in Washington Crossing, Pennsylvania, in particular Darren Kindred, for their interest and support while I played tennis and wrote the book.

Pancho is a world traveler, and friends from Ecuador, England, Australia, South Africa and the United States, among other places, all cherished their time with him and were eager to share their stories with me. Everyone I talked to was delighted that this book was going to be written, making it clear that Pancho Segura has contributed more than most people will ever know, not only to the game of tennis but to the many friends he has amused, captivated, and enriched throughout his life. I thank them all.

The University of Nebraska Press—in particular Rob Taylor, Joeth Zucco, art director Annie Shahan, and freelance copyeditor Karen Brown—were efficient and patient as they shepherded the manuscript through the process of publication. Walter Lippincott worked tirelessly to get the manuscript into the right hands for publication, and it is largely thanks to him that it has seen the light of day under such good auspices.

Finally, I should like to thank David H. Koch for being the original inspiration for this project about the life of Pancho Segura. His support on every level throughout the process was invaluable. Without him, there would be no book.

Appendix From *The Tennis Partner* by Abraham Verghese

Carlsbad, even at midnight, is a golfer's town. The bellboy asks about my golf bag as we putter along narrow paths between manicured lawns on the way to my room. I point to the Samsonite—feather light and rattling on his golf cart—two tennis rackets and little else in it.

"Tennis," I say, weary after a whole day of airports and planes.

I ask the bellboy whether the old man still teaches. Or is he being used as a come-on, illusory, like the spa beauty photographed on the edge of a steaming whirlpool.

"He still teaches," says the bellboy. "He's always there. Giving lessons."

The next morning at seven thirty I call to say I want a lesson. They check his schedule and say, "Possibly." Yes, possibly even today. They will check with him when he comes in. He will call me. Fifteen minutes later, the phone rings while I sip coffee and read the calorie count printed on the breakfast menu. The old man himself is on the line. He pronounces my name carefully.

"I can take you at twelve o'clock," he says. "You want half hour?"

"One hour."

"Okay . . . You know it is a hundred dollars."

"Yes sir," I say.

I check in early at the pro shop. I hear him talk in an office at the back. I watch some doubles on center court, and after a long time—I am very early—I sense him come out. The same voice I heard on the phone—raspy and faintly accented—asks a man sitting near me if he is waiting for a lesson.

"It's me," I say, standing and turning to face him.

He is much shorter than I imagined and absurdly pigeon-toed. After offering me a handshake, he takes off in a brisk crab walk, his trunk swaying from side to side, two rackets clutched under the crook of his arm, head held high despite the stoop of his back that robs him of more inches. He wears white cotton warm-up pants and a predominantly white tennis jacket—zipped, and upturned collar—in which he floats as if in a life vest. A floppy white cap shields his face but not the eagle eyes perched above the pointed nose. His tennis shoes are high-topped, at least two sizes too big and richly padded. The laces are very loose and yet the tongue of the shoe bulges out. I picture the varus forefoot, curled inward, scrunching the last, all the weight on the outer edge of the foot as he waddles.

"How long you been playing tennis?"

(I barely hear him, he is walking so far ahead of me.)

"Twenty years," I say. "Off and on," I add as an afterthought.

If he hears me, he gives no sign. Maybe this is something he asks without paying attention to the answer. I imagine he gets answers like: "I just took it up last week." Or: "I have never played but I love to watch Chrissie Evert."

We are at the court.

"Show me your grips," he says, fingering his own racket.

I show him my forehand—extreme Western. He makes a sucking sound between his teeth and I think I see a grimace. The darkened sun furrows etched on his face are so close to a scowl, it is difficult to tell.

"Now show me the backhand."

Again a contortion of the face suggests he would prefer more Continental.

"The serve now."

I show him a backhand grip.

"Good. Can you slice the backhand?"

"Yes."

"Can you slice the forehand to approach the net?"

". . . Yes."

"Good." He is relieved; I am salvageable. "'Cause you can't approach the net with topspin.

"Listen to me," he says, coming up so close that I tense. "Listen to what I am going to tell you because it is the most important thing about tennis. What's your name? Abraham? Abraham, listen to me, this is what tennis is all about:

"The ball must be hit deep or angled away.

"The short ball must be punished outright—or used to attack.

"The game is won at the net.

"That's it," he says.

He studies me carefully, looking perhaps for doubt, disagreement, or understanding.

I feel a sense of bewilderment. Not that any of these aphorisms—"keep it deep," "attack the short ball," "win at the net"—are new. Yet, at this instant, while I stand on immaculate Har-Tru no different from Har-Tru anywhere, under a pristine Carlsbad sky that could be an Abu Dhabi sky, fingering a racket handle as familiar as a lover's instep under the bedsheet, a lifetime of tennis is temporarily erased and it is as if I am hearing for the first time how the game is played. The mechanical aspects of hitting the ball—head still, knees bent, eyes on the ball, the usual focus of any tennis lesson I have taken in the past—seem banal compared to the philosophy of hitting the ball.

"There is nothing else," he says, as if reading my thoughts. "That's it."

His scrutiny has not ceased. I am shocked at the simplicity of the explanation. It's not to be dismissed, for this is, after all, the man reputed to be the wisest strategist in tennis, the man who made Connors the potent force he is. This is the man who won three NCAA tennis championships, three Pro Singles titles, twice beating Pancho Gonzales.

I feel a warmth from him; perhaps he realizes a catharsis has occurred in the student and what follows for the teacher will be simple denouement. In the depths of the left pupil I see a hint of a cloudy-white opacity, a reminder of the passage of time.

"So now," he says, "we will hit some balls. Some will be short. Hit them and come in. Hit deep and to the center for now."

We begin to rally. It is a feeling akin to communion as his ball, heavy and deliberate, is met by my racket and propelled back, deep, but wobbling eccentrically, revealing a diffidence that diminishes the longer the ball is in play. He hits a short ball—deliberately. I slice a backhand approach—head down, knees bent, follow-through deep to the target—and he effortlessly lobs over my left shoulder and into the backhand corner. It is not its height that makes it unplayable—the ball is behind me before I ever see it.

I go back to the baseline, rally again, approach on a short ball—and the same thing happens. He strikes my approach on the rise; a wonderfully timed half-volley lob hit with a firm wrist and careful follow-through. That lob and his killer two-handed forehand were what he was best known for when he was on the tour. The stroke begins in the misshapen feet and travels up the bowed knees and into the locked hips that are now magically fluid and supple; the completeness of the stroke fuses disparate and inconsonant parts into one synchronous thrust. The ball is struck well out in front, at the apogee of uncoiling—as if the ball were secondary and of less import than the stroke itself. He holds the follow-through, punctuating the stroke, remaining motionless as the ball rises, spinning in the same axis as its flight, over my left shoulder and into the backhand corner that beckons.

"You need to think," he says. "That is what you need to learn. Your strokes are not bad. When you see my racket like this, you know it is a short ball—start coming in at that moment. If you anticipate, you can hit a better approach. Let us keep working on the approach."

He feeds me short balls and I approach. Unless my approach is deep enough to push him onto the back foot, he punishes it with the lob—each one identical to the one before, arching over my backhand and into the corner. I am now so intent on coming in that when he hits a high ball that lands at the baseline and kicks up, accelerating, I make an awkward high swing—more an act of self-preservation than a legitimate stroke—and I pop up a short ball. When I look up, he is two feet inside the service box, appearing out of nowhere. He slaps the ball with a hint of underspin at a sharp angle crosscourt. I hear a guttural *thwump* as the shot comes off his racket; his stroke epitomizes the idea of "put the ball away." I stand lead-footed, watching the ball skid low, graze the inside of the line on its way to set the chain-link fence into song.

"Come here!" he says, slapping the net with his racket edge.

"I knew you were going to hit short before you knew. My ball caught you flat on your heels. You had to hit short! Remember, all tennis shots are played waist-high. You should have moved back to hit that shot. Use your head."

He makes as if to return to the baseline, but thinks better of it and continues:

"If the ball is coming this high over the net, where will it bounce?"

"High and deep," I say.

"So?"

"So I must move back," I say.

"And if it comes in low over the net, like this, where will it bounce?"

"Short."

"So what will you do?"

"Slice and come in."

"Yes. Go back and let us try some more. Short ball, come in."

He walks back to the hamper, picks it up, and hooks it over his shoulder while he extracts seven balls. He sets the hamper down the same way—without flexing his back or bending at the waist. Seeing his effort, I resolve not to waste balls.

More approaches. My heart pounds behind my eyes and sweat soaks my T-shirt and forms a V on the front of my tennis shorts. If the approach is not deep, he punishes it—always with the lob. I begin to recognize the flight path of the lob; a lucent arc carved out of red Carlsbad air.

When I finally hit ten good approaches, he says:

"That is what I want! Come here."

I go to the net, grateful for a respite.

He looks around and lowers his voice: "Of all the pros, John is the best," he says. "For my money, he is the best because he knows how to read the short ball and take advantage. That, my friend, is what it is all about. That is the name of the game.

"Those baseliners—you know who I mean, the kids who just now came along—I'm not saying they cannot make money or that they cannot be good players. But to be great, you have to take the short ball and come in. You have to be an attacking player. You put the pressure on the other guy. You make him make the shot."

Forty minutes have gone by and we have spent most of it on the approach shot. In the next few minutes he looks at all my other shots. He has me volley at the net. He is happy only when I hit the volley with a racket almost perpendicular to the net, angling the ball away acutely and with pace.

"That's the only kind of volley to hit," he says. "You hit your first volley from here," he says, standing two feet inside the service box. "And you angle it to where the guy is not standing. Unless the score is 40–15—in which case you go behind him. If he has a weakness, then go for the weakness. Keep attacking it. Get his momentum going so it carries him off the court."

He looks at my drop volleys.

"Drop volleys are for soft balls only, and they are always hit crosscourt," he says. "Don't try it on a ball that is hit hard. Nobody can do that. Nobody.

"You can't let the ball drop too low before you hit the drop volley. If you let it drop, your opponent knows you have to hit it up. And so he will be coming in. Unless he is stupid.

"If he is stupid, you will win anyway."

We practice the lob. In all the lessons I have ever had, this is the first time I have practiced the lob.

He looks at my serve, return of serve, lob, overhead, and passing shots. He makes only minor comments. I get the feeling he is unconcerned, given the nature of our brief lesson, about trying to correct the mechanisms of a shot. It is the use of the shot that he dwells on:

"The best time to lob," he says, "is on the first volley. Because your opponent's momentum is being moved forward."

I think about the lob over my backhand that he has hit at least sixteen times today.

When the hour is up, I help him pick up balls. He has not broken a sweat under his jacket. We walk back together, me beside him, in stride, in rapture, for I feel I have been given a special insight. I think of the countless times and the many years he has done this, imparted his principles to a student; there is in it a faith and a doggedness that reminds me of the old horse-and-buggy doctor going out season after season in all kinds of weather to see the ill. When he was a top-flight player, trophies and fame were his reward, but now, in the obscurity of this court on the edge of the property, he still puts on a class act every time. I find this inspiring both as a teacher of medicine and as a student of tennis.

In his office, I show him an old picture of my eldest son that I happen to have in the pocket of the racket cover. My son is four and he is in a tennis hat, pointing at the camera, his dimples irresistible. I ask him if he will sign it.

I see the first smile of the day on his face and a hint of tenderness. The teeth are perfectly straight.

"What's his name?" he asks.

He writes painstakingly, laboriously, and as if nothing is more important than this, yet a felt-tipped racket would work better in those knobby hands: "To Steven: Punish the short ball. Pancho Segura."

Bibliography

Braden, Vic, and Robert Wool. *Vic Braden's Mental Tennis: How to Psych Yourself to a Winning Game*. Boston: Little, Brown, 1993.

Canessa Oneto, Mario. *100 Años de Historia del Tenis Ecuatoriano*. Guayaquil, Ecuador: Poligrafica, 2000.

Deford, Frank. *Big Bill Tilden: The Triumphs and the Tragedy*. Toronto: Sport Classic Books, 2004.

Drucker, Joel. *Jimmy Connors Saved My Life*. Toronto: Sport Classic Books, 2004.

Forbes, Gordon. *A Handful of Summers*. New York: Mayflower Books, 1978.

Gonzales, Pancho (as told to Cy Price). *Man with a Racket: The Autobiography of Pancho Gonzales*. London: Thomas Yoseloff, 1959.

Kramer, Jack (with Frank Deford). *The Game: My Forty Years in Tennis*. New York: G.P. Putnam's Sons, 1979.

LeCompte, Tom. *The Last Sure Thing: The Life and Times of Bobby Riggs*. Easthampton MA: Black Squirrel Publishing, 2003.

McCauley, Joe. *The History of Professional Tennis*. Windsor, England: Joe McCauley, reprinted 2003.

Scott, Eugene L. *Fame*. New York: Tennis Week, 1999.

Segura, Pancho (with Gladys Heldman). *Pancho Segura's Championship Strategy: How to Play Winning Tennis*. With an introduction by Billie Jean King. New York: McGraw-Hill, 1976.

Verghese, Abraham. *The Tennis Partner*. New York: HarperCollins, 1998.

Index

Page references in *italics* indicate a photograph; the first part of the reference indicates the page of text the photograph section follows; the second part of the reference indicates the page within the photograph section.

Abramson, Jesse, x
Acuna y Rey, Carlos, 15–16
Adelson, Merv, 148, 150–51, 152, 162, 172. *See also* La Costa
Agassi, Andre, 88, 161–62, 171, 174, 175
Agassi, Rita (Mrs. Richard Gonzales), 88, 161, 174
Aguirre, Juan, 22, 24–25
Alexander, Fred B., 115
Alire, Carmen Esperanza. *See* Gonzales, Carmen Esperanza Alire (Mrs. Manuel Gonzales)
All England Lawn Tennis and Croquet Club, 40, 163
amateur tennis. *See* tennis
"The Amateur" (Tilden), 41
Amritraj, Anand, 176
Anderson, Mal, 100, 101
Andrews, Julie, 117
Annacone, Paul, 176
Annexe Tennis Club, 183

Ann-Margret, 152
Araton, Harvey, 160
Argentina, 17, 19, 20
Arnaz, Desi, Jr., 122, 143, 151, 162, 167
Ashe, Arthur, 146, 175; *Days of Grace*, 101; and Jimmy Connors, 156–58, 159, 160–61; *Off the Court*, 128; and Pancho Gonzales, 128–29
Ashe, Bowman, 34
Association of Tennis Professionals, 157, 176
Attlee, Clement, 55
Ayala, Luis, 104

Bacall, Lauren, 117, *120/17–18*
Bacharach, Burt, 117, 152, 156
Bachmann, Larry, 115
"Battle of the Sexes," 43, 76, 155, 168. *See also* Riggs, Bobby
Beggs, Alexi, 168
Beggs, Viktoria, 168–71, 173
Betz, Pauline, 76–77, 116, 134
Beverly Hills Tennis Club, 68, 106, 111, 114–30, 132–33, 146–47, 162; founding of the, 114–16; Jimmy Connors at the, 139–40, 142; popularity of, among young people, 122–27;

130, 152, 164–65, 172; and
daughter Maria, 125–26;
relationship of, with Spencer
Segura, 110
Segura, Francisco. *See* Segura,
Pancho
Segura, Maria, 125–26, 165, 172
Segura, Pancho, 69, 134; awards
won by, 176; at the Beverly
Hills Tennis Club, 106, 111,
114–15, 116–30, *120/11*, *120/16*,
120/18–20, *120/25*, 132–33, 139–
40, 146–48; birth of, 2; and the
Bolivarian Olympics, 15–17; and
the Bruckmann Burtons, 11–13;
and celebrities, 116–17, 118–19,
120/11, *120/16–21*, *120/23*, *120/25*,
121, 128, 129–30, 146, 151–52,
171; childhood illnesses of,
3–5; childhood of, 4–8, *40/1–2*;
as *cholo* (mixed blood), 2;
coaches Andre Agassi, 161–62,
171; coaches Jimmy Connors,
120/11–14, 136–42, 144–46, 153–
62, 177–78; and discrimination,
vii, 13–14, 80–81, 101, 110, 128;
divorce of, from Virginia Smith,
105, 107, 109–10; and driving,
54, 98; and early training, 2,
5–11; and earnings, 19–20,
28–29, 50, 95, 98, 117–18,
146–47, 152; and Ecuadorian
government support, 28–30;
family and siblings of, 3, 6–8,
9–10, 19–20, *40/3*, 47–48,
95, *120/26*, 165, 183–84; first
tournaments of, in America,
24–28; friendship of, with

Bobby Riggs, 25; friendship
of, with Richard Gonzales,
74, 79–81, 82–83, 84–85, 87,
88, 89–91, 99, *120/5*, 127–28,
174; and godfather Don Juan
José Medina, 4–5, 9; and the
Guayaquil Tennis Club, 5, 7,
9–11, 13–15, 17, *120/26*; journey
of, to the United States,
21–23; and knowledge of the
game, 111–14, 123, 137–38,
140, 153, 169–71, 191; at La
Costa, 148, 149, 151–55, 156,
161–62, 164–69, 171–75; legacy
of, 178–84; marriage of, to
Beverley Young, 105, 107–9,
110, *120/22*, 125–26, 164–65;
marriage of, to Virginia Smith,
40/8, 45, 47–48, 54, 93–95, 96,
98–99, 105, 107; matches of,
with Richard Gonzales, vii–x,
78, 85, 89–91, 113, 163–64; and
the NCAA Intercollegiate singles
championship, 36, 38; in New
York City, 28–31; nicknames of,
vii, viii, 58, 80, 98, 112; *Pancho
Segura's Championship Strategy*,
160–61; patrons of, 11–13,
30–32, 48; physical description,
vii, 1, 4; playing style of, viii–x,
8, 16, 18, 25, 27, 28, *40/12–13*,
56–58, 78, 97, 103, 176; and
politics, 55; and private lessons,
118, 119, 122, 147; on the pro
tour, *40/14–18*, 44–45, 49–60,
73, 75–80, 85–92, 96–103, 105–
6, 107–8, *120/2–3*, *120/6*; and
racial discrimination, vii,

Sugar Bowl, 33

Talbert, Bill, 33, 38, 70
Tanner, Roscoe, 141
Taylor, Robert, 116
Taylor, Roger, 132
El Telegrafo, 38; and the
    Bolivarian Olympics, 16, 17;
    and nationalistic language,
    19; Rodriguez Garzon article,
    10–11; and Segura's departure
    for America, 21
Temple, Shirley, 120/21
tennis: amateur *vs.* professional,
    40–45, 49, 96–97, 100, 104;
    and anti-semitism, 115; elitist
    culture of, 4–5, 49, 83, 101;
    lawn, 40; open, 49, 104,
    130–31, 152; popularity of, 104,
    152–53, 154, 155–56, 162; pro
    tour economics, 41, 42, 45, 49,
    50–53, 59, 76–77, 100, 104–5;
    and the Van Alen Simplified
    Scoring System (VASS), 89–90;
    and women players, 41, 75–77,
    155, 168
Tennis Hall of Fame, 176
Tennis Magazine, 73, 159–60, 180
The Tennis Partner (Verghese),
    172; excerpt, 189–95
Thompson, Al, 134
Thompson, Bertha ("Two-Mom"),
    134, 135, 136, 143–44. *See also*
    Connors, Jimmy
Thompson, Gloria. *See* Connors,
    Gloria
Tilden, Bill ("Big Bill"), viii, 41–
    42, 43, 44, 65, 69, 82, 115

Todd, Lisa, 167
Tournament of Champions,
    97–98
Trabert, Tony, 78, 81, 96, 97–98,
    101, 108, 120/2–3
Tracy, Spencer, 130

Union Club, 3, 115, 182
University of Miami, 33, 34–37,
    40/7
Uraga, Don Nelson, 8
Uruguayan Tennis Federation,
    18
U.S. Clay Court championship,
    38, 71, 78
U.S. Grass Court Pro Champion-
    ship, 78, 104
U.S. Lawn Tennis Championship,
    69
U.S. Nationals, 38
U.S. Open, 71–73, 111, 127, 153,
    157, 160, 177–78
U.S. Professional Champion-
    ships, 61, 78

Van Alen, Jimmy, 89
Van Alen Simplified Scoring
    System (VASS), 89–90
Vanderbilt, Cornelius, 116
van Dillen, Erik, 141, 145
Van Horn, Welby, 43
Verghese, Abraham: *The Tennis
    Partner*, 172, 189–95
Vic Braden Tennis College, 101
Villa, Pancho, vii, 80
Vines, Ellsworth, 42, 97, 115–16,
    175